HAPPINESS
IN AMERICA

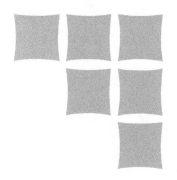

HAPPINESS IN AMERICA

A CULTURAL HISTORY

LAWRENCE R. SAMUEL

ROWMAN & LITTLEFIELD
Lanham • Boulder • New York • London

DEC 1 3 2018

Published by Rowman & Littlefield
An imprint of The Rowman & Littlefield Publishing Group, Inc.
4501 Forbes Boulevard, Suite 200, Lanham, Maryland 20706
www.rowman.com

Unit A, Whitacre Mews, 26-34 Stannary Street, London SE11 4AB

British Library Cataloguing in Publication Information Available

Library of Congress Cataloging-in-Publication Data Available

ISBN: 978-1-5381-1579-4 (cloth : alk. paper)
ISBN: 978-1-5381-1577-0 (electronic)

♾™ The paper used in this publication meets the minimum requirements of American National Standard for Information Sciences—Permanence of Paper for Printed Library Materials, ANSI/NISO Z39.48-1992.

Printed in the United States of America

To Freya, who brought me joy

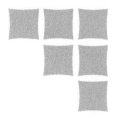

CONTENTS

PREFACE

I **used to** be a happy guy. For me, happiness revolved around the freedom to do pretty much whatever I wanted whenever I wanted. At fifty years old, with no family of my own or real job to speak of, I could pursue any and all avenues of happiness of my own design without worrying about the consequences that otherwise usually come with a focus on oneself. Writing during the day and partying at night was a perfect recipe for happiness for me, a wonderful fusion of intellectualism and hedonism. Maintaining this lifestyle required avoiding those two party-poopers of happiness—responsibility and commitment—but that was a skill I had mastered over the course of decades with dedicated practice.

And then—whoosh—it was all over. A girlfriend, child, and wife (in that order) squashed my personal interpretation of happiness like a bug, with the massive quantities of freedom I had possessed for so many years now just a literal happy memory. Do I have any regrets about this precipitous drop in my happiness quotient? None at all. Filling the void of happiness has been an equally voluminous amount of joy, which for me is a much different kind of emotion. Joy is a deeper, richer experience than happiness, I argue, and something that can only come with close relationships with other people (and perhaps with pets and other living things). Love is an essential ingredient of joy, I think, something not necessarily true of happiness. As well, achieving joy is possible only by allowing those two bugaboos of happiness, responsibility and commitment, to come into one's life, a lesson most people learn in their twenties and thirties.

Although it was by no means planned, dwelling in happiness for my first two acts of life and joy in my third has worked out very well, I've come to believe, with the leap I made necessary in order for me to evolve as a human being. As I wrote in my previous books *American Fatherhood* and *Aging in America*, being an older dad has dovetailed nicely with the sense of contentment that often comes with aging, with these two major life changes creating a powerful synergy of joy at the expense of happiness. While I miss the unpredictability and independence that came with my happy life, my joyful life more than makes up for it. It would be great to have both, of course, but for me at least the two emotions appear to be largely mutually exclusive. This is my personal story and I make no judgments on others' life choices, I need to point out, as each of us has to follow our own path.

I tell this story for two reasons. The first is to make it clear that the meaning of happiness is an entirely subjective affair (i.e., one that is individually, personally, and somehow uniquely defined). This is a theme that resonates throughout the history of happiness in America. The second reason that I think my personal story helps set up the main body of this book is to differentiate between happiness and joy, a distinction that I believe is much more than semantics. (Oddly, to me, anyway, no such distinction between happiness and joy was made in any of the hundreds of articles and books I read to produce this project, with one notable exception that is discussed in the epilogue.) Happiness is maddeningly difficult to define, we hear over and over again, and an elusive, fleeting emotion that is as slippery as an eel to catch and hang onto. Joy, however, is a universal emotion, meaning it is essentially the same for everyone and one of the few things all of us share in some way. While a history of joy in America would certainly make an interesting book, this one is about happiness, the "subjective state of emotional well-being" that many smart people have over the years attempted to understand. I hope this work makes some contribution to that worthy endeavor.

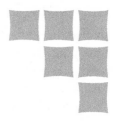

INTRODUCTION

Clap along, as Pharrell Williams put it in his #1 song of 2014, "Happy," if you know what happiness is to you. Many Americans have not had success in finding what happiness means to them, a major reason why I wrote this book and why I think it's worth reading. *Happiness in America* is, as its title and subtitle make clear, a cultural history of happiness in the United States. No such book exists, a surprising thing given the prominent role that the idea and pursuit of happiness has played in this country since we became a country. Much interest currently revolves around happiness in America (and around the world), so much so that one could reasonably argue that there is a "happiness movement" afoot. *Happiness in America* fills this literary and scholarly gap by charting the course of happiness within American culture over the past century, in the process shedding further light on our national identity and character.

The wide range of arenas in which happiness intersects reflects the subject's centrality in everyday life in America these past one hundred years. Happiness overlaps with psychology, science, religion and spirituality, business, medicine and health, relationships, philosophy, sociology, child raising, politics, and technology, making the work truly multi- and interdisciplinary. Rather than follow a linear path, happiness has bobbed and weaved over the decades, this book shows, its arc or trajectory a twisting and unpredictable one. Happiness has also both shaped and reflected our core values, with its expression at any given time a key indicator of who we are as a people. This book thus adds a missing and valuable piece to our understanding of American culture, and aspires to be recognized as a seminal resource dedicated to all things happiness.

Beyond serving as the definitive guide to happiness in this country, *Happiness in America* offers readers a provocative argument that challenges standard thinking. Despite popular belief, Americans have never been a particularly happy people, the work demonstrates, with abundant anecdotal evidence and hard research backing up that bold claim. Our perpetual search for happiness indicates widespread dissatisfaction and discontent with life in general, something that will come as a surprise to many. The image of Americans as a happy-go-lucky people is thus more mythology than reality, an important finding rooted in the inherent flaws of consumer capitalism. Our competitive and comparative American Way of Life has not proven to be an especially good formula for happiness, I argue, with external signs of success unlikely to produce appreciably happier people. Rather, happiness has more often come from being in and appreciating the moment, this book shows, an idea that has major implications for how all of us might approach our lives in the future.

That happiness has been central to the American idea and experience for the past century is reason enough why its story is worth telling. (Ask any American what he or she wants most in life and the majority will say to be happy.) The pursuit of happiness—a phrase penned by the Founding Fathers in the Declaration of Independence—has served as a primary ambition for many Americans in the nation's history, especially during the past century. It was immediately after World War I when the modern concept of happiness was born, I posit, making the 1920s a good place to begin the story. Happiness became a louder and louder part of the national conversation over the years, riding on the greater interest in psychology and the expansion of that field, especially as related to personality. Despite myriad social, economic, and political factors including the crossing over into a new century and millennium, an aging population, a technological revolution, and the entry of large institutions and major corporations on the scene, the degree of happiness in America has not budged for as long as it has been measured.

Of course, the United States has held no monopoly on the pursuit of happiness. Throughout history, as Darrin M. McMahon showed in his *Happiness: A History*, Nicholas P. White in his *A Brief History of Happiness*, and Sissela Bok in her *Exploring Happiness: From Aristotle to Brain Science*, some of the greatest minds of the day have weighed in on the subject.[1] Needless to say, happiness remains a mainstay of the enormously popular self-help industry, with boatloads of books published (many of them bestsellers) outlining how readers can become happier people. Recent ones such as Matthieu Ricard's *Happiness: A Guide to Developing Life's Most Important Skill* (2006), Gretchen Rubin's *The Happiness Project: Or, Why I Spent a Year Trying to Sing in the Morning, Clean My Closets, Fight Right, Read Aristotle, and Generally Have More Fun* (2009), and Neil Pasricha's *The Happiness Equation: Want Nothing + Do Anything = Have Everything* (2016) have each offered paths by which readers can increase their happiness quotient, adding to the abundant body of literature in the field.[2] Despite all this smart thinking and inspired musing (not to mention a fair amount of scholarly research in recent times), it's safe to say that the code to happiness has not been cracked. Great wisdom dedicated to the subject has not revealed any secret formula to happiness, in other words, leading one to the reasonable conclusion that there simply isn't one.

Americans are considered to be a generally happy people, both among themselves and by foreigners, this story shows, but the story of happiness in this country is not an especially pretty one. Self-doubt, insecurity, and uncertainty have been tightly woven into the narrative of happiness, a major source of frustration for those seeking to be happier people. In conjunction with our achievement- and money-oriented society that is often the source of what Alain de Botton called "status anxiety," the belief that we are a chosen people and a shining example to others around the world to follow has set too high of a bar of happiness for most individuals to actually realize.[3] Our core mythologies grounded in specialness and superiority have been instrumental in leading Americans to assume they are entitled or have an inherent right to happiness, the basis for a rude surprise when life does not turn out that way. Our expectations for happiness have far exceeded its realization, in other words, suggesting our way of life rooted in consumer capitalism has major flaws in terms of emotional fulfillment. In a nutshell, happiness has proven to be an elusive and often futile pursuit in this country over the last century, something that has held true across the social divisions of race, gender, and class.

Alongside the many personal stories describing individuals' struggle to find happiness, numerous polls, surveys, and questionnaires have made it clear that Americans are not the happy people they have been popularly believed to be. Until the 1970s, when happiness can be said to have become a legitimate field within psychology, studies consistently overstated how happy Americans claimed to be. Poor research methodologies, and probably a good dose of national pride, gave the appearance that upward of 90 percent of Americans were happy people. Better research over the past few decades has shown that the number is far lower, however, hard evidence that happiness is a relatively scarce commodity in this country. Ratings of happiness among different countries have consistently suggested the same. The United States currently ranks eighteenth in national happiness, in between Luxembourg and the United Kingdom, according to the 2018 World Happiness Report, with Finland topping the list.[4] Members of the "Greatest Generation," baby boomers, millennials, and postmillennials have defined happiness in their own terms, but none of these generations can be considered to be a truly happy bunch based on their own reports.

Americans' uneasy relationship with happiness has escalated over the last century, with our more affluent society and bountiful marketplace not leading to a nation full of mostly happy people. In fact, the broader desire for the good things in life has fueled greater disappointment, discontent, and dissatisfaction when happiness didn't result from wealth, power, or some other externally defined, other-directed measure of success. Not surprisingly, hundreds if not thousands of experts have over the years capitalized on Americans' perceived happiness deficiency by offering advice on how they could become happier people. Happiness has represented a major and growing segment of the how-to and self-help business, although there is little evidence to suggest that any particular approach has actually worked. Marketers too have seized Americans' deep desire to be happy by positioning their products and services as agents of happiness. The art of happiness gradually shifted to more of a science over the years, backed up by research showing there was a biological component to the emotion or state of mind. Today, one's relative level of happiness is seen primarily as a function of brain chemistry and genetic predisposition, propelling neuroscience and bio-engineering to the frontiers of the field.

The irony in writing a book about happiness that is more about the lack of happiness has not been overlooked. Americans' ambitious, perhaps even desperate search for happiness has been a remarkably democratic one. No segment of the population has been excluded, with studies showing time and time again that social and economic divisions such as income, education, intelligence, and religion matter little in determining one's level of happiness. Researchers have pulled happiness apart every which way over the past century in the attempt to establish a scientific basis for the fledgling field, but these efforts have been largely in vain. Relatedly, individuals' happiness has been little affected by the wide cultural swings the nation has experienced since the end of World War I. Boom or bust, war or peace, turmoil or tranquility, liberal or conservative in the White House—Americans' happiness has proven to be largely resilient to the constant shifting of our social and economic plates.

Not surprisingly, given the complexity and enigmatic nature of the emotion, happiness has proved to be a very challenging subject for researchers in the field to try to understand. Researchers have asked the same questions over the decades, with the answers still not clear. Does a happy childhood produce a happy adult? (Sometimes.) Were people in the past happier than today? (Perhaps.) Is happiness more a function of environmental factors or the individual mind? (Some say the latter, others the former.) Is unhappiness the opposite of happiness? (Apparently not, strangely enough, with some studies showing that each emotion has a range or spectrum all of its own.) What is happiness, anyway? (A subjective state of well-being, according to most experts.)

Further complicating matters has been the bias critics have shown when examining happiness. Sociologists have viewed happiness through the lens of society, psychologists the mind, physicians the body, preachers one's faith, politicians the government, and so on. This has made the field a jumble or hodgepodge of viewpoints, more so I believe than most other subjects. As well, all sorts of experts have attempted to control or take ownership of happiness in America in some way, this too contributing to the scattered nature of the subject. Businesspeople, government officials, and religious leaders have seen themselves as arbiters of happiness and have assumed responsibility for delivering it to Americans in order to solidify their own power. Likewise, politicians from each persuasion have often claimed to be the greater instrument of happiness than their competitors, making it appear that the emotion can be bestowed rather than earned.[5]

Much attention has been paid to the relationship of happiness to another thing of great interest to most Americans: money. It has been generally believed that happiness is strongly correlated with prosperity, both personal and national, but this too has turned out to be a generally false assumption. A different set of challenges emerges with upward mobility, anyone who has experienced it can tell you, with much evidence to suggest that both wealth and success may improve one's quality of life but are not likely to produce a happier person. To that point, if there is a single thing to know about the relationship between happiness and money, it is that the latter typically cannot purchase the former. Despite what Madison Avenue has told us, happiness is not for sale, something that both marketers and consumers are determined to ignore. As with any positive development in life, a new thing or experience may increase one's happiness quotient, but it will undoubtedly be a relatively brief bump versus a sustained rise. Our consumerist society has thus led many a happiness seeker astray, with advertisers routinely dangling the emotion like a carrot before us. While the product or service may indeed offer some pleasure or contentment, any measure of genuine happiness will not be forthcoming as the feeling simply does not translate into materialistic or experiential terms and vice versa.

Given all this, one has to question Americans' inclination to work harder to make more money in order to become happier. Inscribed in our national charter, happiness is no doubt a very American idea, but the ways in which most of us pursue it are not very well suited to creating it. Our system of free market capitalism (the American Way of Life) and aspirational ethos (the American Dream) are actually better designed to generate stress than happiness, I believe, with the pressures of modern life not conducive to promoting a state of well-being.[6] Those who have dropped out of the "rat race" are more likely to find a sense of inner peace, history shows, implying that our competitive society is at best not ideal and at worst fundamentally flawed in terms of seeding the possibility of happiness.

While happiness is of course a timeless subject and universal in scope, Americans have had a special relationship with it since the nation's founding. This relationship accelerated in the twentieth century with the expansion of the middle class, the emergence of mass culture, and the shift in work from factory jobs and farming to managerial positions.[7] Broader prosperity not only raised Americans' expectations to be happy but at the same time increased the social pressure to be so, a push-pull effect triggered by the forces of modernism. Happiness as we know it today can thus be seen as a luxury of the modern age, as prior to that humans spent much of their time and energy simply trying to survive as long as possible.

Like most luxuries, however, the pursuit of happiness over the past century has come at a high cost. As the very selective editing of one's life on Facebook in order to create a narrative of happiness suggests, there remains significant social pressure for individuals to be perceived as happy. Social media has immeasurably intensified this pressure, triggering what many experts believe is a true psychological crisis among young people. Being judged by others as an unhappy person carries a certain kind of social stigma in this country, as such individuals are generally seen as failures for not taking advantage of their inalienable right to happiness. There is little doubt that happiness is a valuable form of cultural currency, more valuable in fact than money that can be easily earned and spent.

A variety of factors have contributed to the elevation of happiness to nearly religious proportions in the United States and most Americans' inability to actually achieve that state of being. We spend way too much time looking back and looking forward, for one thing, with the all-important present often obscured by regrets about the past and concern for the future. Our dominant Judeo-Christian religions are also not very happiness-friendly, one can argue, as they are significantly more judgmental than the let-it-be philosophies of Buddhism and other Eastern spiritualities. On an even more basic level, most of us have simply not been taught or shown how to be happy as, until the relatively recent appearance of positive psychology, there is rarely if ever any training or instruction in the subject. The focus of both education and socialization is on learning how to be successful in a particular field, the assumption being that that will lead to happiness. That assumption is wrong, however, with many an American surprised when happiness does not come his or her way after achieving his or her professional or personal goals.

Despite the very real possibility that true happiness is simply beyond the capacity of many of us because of environmental factors, neural wiring, or some combination of each, a huge business has been built around Americans' aggressive pursuit of it. Happiness is a skill or technique that one can master with enough practice, we've been told repeatedly, standard advice within the self-improvement, self-help, and now "personal development" industry. Such inspirational and motivational coaxing offers the sense that we are in control of our emotional destiny, an empowering idea that not surprisingly has proved immensely popular. Happiness is a choice, according to most how-tos, a decision for individuals to make if they have the courage and temerity to do so. (Someone once actually told me, "One day I just decided to be happy." Another acquaintance was delighted to inform me he "went from a 2 to an 8," the numbers referring to how much happier he had become after relocating.) Women's magazines have contributed mightily to the body of how-to literature dedicated to happiness, often packaging it like a crash diet or step program that can be successfully accomplished in a matter of a few days or weeks. Women's pursuit of happiness in America is a story of its own, with assigned gender roles and blatant discrimination playing a major role in their quest to be happier people.

Alongside the abundance of fluffier advice that has further established the notion that happiness is just around the corner if one just knew where to look for it, a generous supply of sound thinking related to the subject has also come forth over the years. Happiness is a holistic experience, some have astutely pointed out, meaning achieving it requires a confluence of mind, body, and soul. One can't catch it, others have sensibly argued, with happiness to bless only those who allow it, like one's muse, to come to oneself on its own accord. Many have wisely suggested that happiness is a social enterprise rather than an individual one, and that only a communal approach to life will lead to its arrival. Relatedly, enabling the happiness of others is the best way to find it within oneself, a learning that often comes with age. It truly is better to give than receive, it appears, a good example of the folk wisdom that has surrounded happiness for millennia. And rather than be a kind of heaven on Earth where one is greeted by an angelic choir, happiness is firmly entrenched in the firmament of everyday life. It really is the little things in life that matter most, in other words, with appreciating every moment one of the keys to being a happy person. It's a cliché, of course, but happiness does indeed seem to be a journey versus a destination, and a way of seeing the world rather than a desired state of being.

Needless to say, Thomas Jefferson did not have such New Agey insights on his mind when he penned the words "the pursuit of happiness" in the Declaration of Independence in 1776. Historians have paid special attention to Jefferson's choice of words or, more accurately, his bold and surprising decision to use the word "happiness" in the document. The phrase is "as fundamental, as baffling, as confused and as interesting an idea as ever appeared in a state paper," thought Howard Mumford Jones of Harvard University, who used *The Pursuit of Happiness* as the title of a series of lectures given at the University of Michigan in 1952 and as the title of a book published the following year. While happiness remained at the center of American political and religious life from the late eighteenth century to the mid-twentieth century, the meaning of the word continually changed, this the thing that Jones found so intriguing.[8] The Zelig-like and even mysterious nature of the term is still very much with us. "Like love," Andrew Delbanco wrote of happiness in 2000, "it is a word that evokes for each of us some private memory or hope that cannot be fully disclosed to others."[9]

While Jefferson is often credited for originating the phrase, it was actually a Virginian colleague of his, George Mason, who is widely acknowledged as having planted the seed. "Pursuing and obtaining happiness and safety" was a basic human right, Mason declared at the Virginia Convention of May 1776, with that phrase included in the preamble of that state's constitution. Jefferson obviously found the phrase compelling but edited it to concentrate its linguistic impact, and attached it to the other inalienable rights of "life and liberty" (here borrowing from the English philosopher John Locke, who some consider to be "the grandfather of the American Declaration of Independence").[10]

Over the next century, most states adopted versions of "the pursuit of happiness in their own constitutions," Mumford explained, further weaving the concept into the American quilt. Happiness is thus a literally stated goal of government in the United States, a remarkable thing from a historical sense that reflects the transcendent vision of the Founding Fathers.[11] "All human beings may come equipped with the pursuit-of-happiness impulse—the urge to find lusher land just over the hill, fatter buffalo in the next valley," observed Jeffrey Kluger, Alex Aciman, and Katy Steinmetz in *Time* in 2013, "but it's Americans who have codified the idea, written it into the Declaration of Independence and made it a central mandate of the national character."[12] "Human equality and the liberty to build a happy life are inextricably linked in the cadences of the Declaration, and thus in America's idea of itself," echoed historian Jon Meacham that same year.[13]

In their 1976 *The American Testament*, William Gorman and Mortimer Adler pointed out that Jefferson's interest in adopting the phrase went far beyond its rhetorical power. Liberal philosophers of the seventeenth and eighteenth centuries like John Locke considered "property" to be one of an individual's fundamental rights, making that term the more likely one for Jefferson to have employed. Jefferson recognized that "happiness" was a more universal and nobler concept than "property," however, and that the pursuit of the latter was ultimately about the pursuit of the former.[14] Happiness went far beyond the ability the ownership of property (or related terms such as "possessions" or "estate"), the Founding Fathers understood, something many Americans would learn a couple centuries later when their materialistic ways did not make them appreciably happier people. "It was a remarkably succinct expression of the American Dream, a confident look to the future rather than a backward nod to John Locke," suggested Timothy J. Shannon, a historian at Gettysburg College, in 2016, thinking that the phrase "remains foundational to how we define ourselves as a nation."[15]

While Jefferson's choice of words was undoubtedly brilliant and courageous (if not entirely original, which he never claimed it to be), treading into the waters of happiness invited the ambiguity that has always been associated with the word. Rather than be limited to the opportunity to pursue one's personal interests without interference by church or state, which was perhaps Jefferson's intent, "the pursuit of happiness" became open to an infinite array of meanings. Regrettably, the phrase could be interpreted as endorsing one's self-interests at the expense of others, certainly not what the man had in mind. Was Jefferson being intentionally inexplicit in opting for "happiness" over "property," allowing for Americans to decide for themselves what the word meant for them? Or did he just not anticipate that the term would prove to be a major source of perplexity, even for constitutional scholars? Going further, did Jefferson mean individual happiness or a collective version designed to serve the public good? No one knows the answers to such questions, leaving the matter as one of the great puzzles in American history.[16]

If the meaning of the word itself is unclear, there is no question that the Founding Fathers recognized how important happiness was to an individual and to society as a whole. "For the Founders, 'happiness' was the obvious word to use because it was obvious to them that the pursuit of happiness is at the center of man's existence," Charles Murray wrote in his 1988 *In Pursuit of Happiness and Good Government*, locating the phrase firmly at the heart of the fundamental American idea. Again, however, it was the role of government to enable happiness among its citizens, the Founders firmly believed, as only that would entice people to consent to be governed.[17] Infused by the thinking and values of the Enlightenment, the Declaration of Independence propelled the trajectory of happiness, canonized its pursuit, and, ultimately, turned it into a primary ambition among most Americans.

In his 2012 article "The History of Happiness" for the *Harvard Business Review*, Peter N. Stearns locates the rise of happiness in the late eighteenth century as a direct result of the cultural atmosphere stirred up by the Enlightenment. Many factors were at work, he acknowledges, but it was "the intellectual shift toward a higher valuation of matters in this world and a reduced commitment to traditional Christian staples such as original sin" that created the climate for happiness to blossom in the Western world. Through the nineteenth century, happiness worked its way into the nooks and crannies of everyday life in America, further establishing it as a desirable emotion for an individual to possess. Happiness could be found at work, the rapidly growing number of middle-class Americans were coming to believe, and family life too was perceived as an opportunity for both adults and children to be happy. Even death would not necessarily impede Americans' pursuit of happiness. "The idea gained ground that heaven was a happy place marked by, among other things, blissful reunions with departed family members," Stearns explained, the afterlife now part of "the ascending culture of happiness."[18]

While this elevation of happiness in America was nothing short of remarkable from a historical sense, it was actually only the beginning of much bigger things to come. "There was yet another surge, particularly in the United States, from the 1920s onward," Stearns continued, as a giant business grew around "the importance of being happy and the personal responsibility to gain happiness." This is where our own story begins, as Jefferson's pithy phrase spawned into such cultural artifacts as the "Happy Birthday" song (1926), the smiley face (1963), McDonald's Happy Meal (1977), and the full-fledged culture of happiness that we have today. Beyond all the how-tos, instructions in and expressions of happiness are nearly everywhere you look today, from Muzak to the television laugh-track to overtly cheerful salespeople to anything bearing the Disney brand.[19] Happiness has found a comfortable home in the Digital Age, with the grinning selfie and the shiny, happy people who populate Facebook and other social media prime examples of how the emotion retains much cultural currency.

Happiness in America tells its story chronologically, beginning at the end of World War I and going right up to today. The spine of the book relies on contemporary, popular magazines (as a cultural history should), as well as scholarly journals and other books. Hundreds of different sources are used, drawing from journalists' and scholars' writing of "the first draft of history." The first chapter of the book, "New Roads to Happiness, 1920–1939," explores the role of happiness in American culture between the world wars, when the idea of happiness became a significantly louder part of the national conversation as Americans looked to a brighter, peaceful future. Chapter 2, "The Paradox of Happiness, 1940–1959," takes readers along the rollercoaster ride that was happiness during the wartime and postwar years, and chapter 3, "What Makes You Happy? 1960–1979," examines happiness in America in the volatile 1960s and 1970s. Chapter 4, "Don't Worry, Be Happy, 1980–1999," discusses the role of happiness in America in the 1980s and 1990s, and chapter 5, "Are You Happy Yet? 2000–2009," shows how the pursuit of happiness picked up further speed in the new century and millennium. The final chapter, "Happily Ever After, 2010–," charts the territory of happiness in recent years, when the emotion is arguably more in demand than ever. While this is by no means a self-help book, I thought it would be a worthwhile exercise to distill the major findings from the abundance of research and insights in the field to offer readers some advice at the end of the book. It would be a shame to not translate into practical terms the efforts of dozens of researchers and other smart people who mined the terrain of happiness over the past century, I reckoned, so feel free to use the material in the epilogue as you wish.

NEW ROADS TO
HAPPINESS, 1920–1939

Today there isn't a movement which isn't infected
with happiness. —Felix Adler, 1931

I n February 1928, a case was filed in New York City's Federal Court that plainly revealed the linguistic power of the term "happiness." Lawyers for the Happiness Candy Stores, a popular retail chain in the New York metropolitan area, were seeking to restrain a competitor from calling itself the Happiness Drug Shops and from using the word "Happiness" in its name. The plaintiff had registered its name back in 1922, the attorneys explained in court, and later registered the name "Fountain of Happiness." More than $2 million had been invested in promoting the two names, according to counsel, and the rival's use of a similar name would confuse customers into thinking they were shopping at Happiness Candy Stores when they were not. Lawyers for the company were asking the court to not just stop Happiness Drug Shops from using that name but for damages, making it clear that it was they who owned the term "Happiness" when it came selling candy, fountain drinks, and tea.[1]

Even if it was just the name of a candy store, happiness was in con-siderable demand in between-the-world-wars America. Immediately after World War I, the idea of happiness became a significantly louder part of the national conversation as Americans looked to a brighter, more peaceful future. Modernity was sweeping across Western culture with a vengeance, in the process raising people's expectations regard-ing happiness. "Are we a happy people?" asked *Harper's* in 1922, with some questioning whether the escalating pace of life and intensifying consumer culture were making Americans more content or less so.[2] Consistent with the science-based rationalism of the Machine Age, happiness was perceived as something that should be "practiced," a skill that could be acquired with dedicated effort. Finding happiness at work—a rather revolutionary notion from a historical sense—became a common pursuit, a reflection of the greater recognition of psychology in the twenties. All in all, there were "new roads to happiness," *World's Work* magazine proposed that same year, considering the opportunities to realize emotional fulfillment were never greater.[3]

The Joy of Living

While the chances to be happy were arguably at an all-time high given the new freedoms to be had by both men and women, it was clear that many Americans were struggling in their individual pursuit of happi-ness. Evidence showed that public school teachers in New York City, for example, were less than happy people in the early 1920s. Teachers earned good salaries at the time, especially for women, but city officials were finding it difficult to attract qualified applicants, even after offering more money for the job. What exactly was the problem with teaching? "Young people simply will not enlist in the numbers and ability needed for a service that does not radiate the joy of living," explained an edu-cator, the rough-and-tumble nature of some of the schools in that city making many a teacher question her choice of occupation. (The prob-lem still exists today in many parts of the country.) "Schools can not be the foundation of liberty and Americanism unless teachers surpass the rest of us in possessing and expressing happiness," the city official stated, calling for "happiness surveys" that would shed additional light on the problem and perhaps reveal possible ways to fix it.[4]

American women of this era would apparently look anywhere and everywhere if it offered the chance of realizing greater happiness. The 1920s were a golden age for supernaturalism, a function in part of the grief many faced due to the loss of loved ones from the world war and 1918 influenza epidemic.[5] Many women looked to the mystical world to try to come to terms with their grief and, in the process, to become a happy person. In 1923, for example, seven hundred women flocked to hear a lecture given at the Hotel Astor in New York City by one Frederick L. Rawson, a self-proclaimed spiritual healer and metaphysician, in hopes they would learn what was promised as the "miracle of perfect happiness." Rawson had already been exposed as a fraud in his home country of England after his scheme to extract gold from the sea failed to produce profits for investors. Still, the man claimed he held the key to happiness, reason enough for the women to raptly listen to every word he had to say on the subject.[6]

Although he did not reveal his secret at the free talk, Rawson did promise to disclose the truth at subsequent lectures costing $1 (about $14 in today's money) or "in private consultations," enough incentive for many in the crowd to be swayed. Achieving happiness appeared to involve ridding oneself of "a mist before the mind," he hinted, an idea that many of the women said they found "beautiful," albeit difficult to understand.[7] Hundreds of women, some of them traveling halfway across the country, returned to the hotel with dollar bills in their hands the following week, eager to learn the "miracle of perfect happiness" from Rawson. Sadly, the miracle would not be revealed, as the man had suddenly died from pneumonia.[8]

Those thinking that happiness resided in learning some of the secrets of life would have another chance to find out just a couple of months later, however. New Yorkers packed into Town Hall to hear what the French chemist M. Emile Coue had to say on the matters of health and happiness, intrigued by what they had heard or read about his technique of "conscious autosuggestion." Unlike Rawson, Coue made it clear he had no miraculous powers, simply wanting to show how those who were unhappy because they suffered from physical ailments could heal themselves by transferring unconscious thoughts into their consciousness. Clearly trading on Freudian psychoanalytic theory, which was all the rage at the time, Coue argued that there was a link between the mind and body, a notion that would become widely accepted within the medical community in the decades ahead.[9] One had considerable control over how happy one was or wasn't, Coue implied, with even those with debilitating diseases able to determine their emotional state of being with proper mental training.[10]

While individuals were believed to be capable of charting their own emotional course if they had the right skills, experts agreed that social problems played a major role in shaping people's health and happiness. A 1925 report from the Columbia University Medical School found that such causes as "domestic disharmony" negatively impacted both physical and mental health, the basis for its recommendation that visiting nurses closely monitor families in which such cases took place. "Every phase of [a family's] life must be under supervision, correction and control," the report stated, "as the health and happiness of the individual depend necessarily upon those of the group." Interestingly, the school found that "the same griefs hit rich and poor," meaning wealth was not a significant factor in determining who was happy and healthy and who was not. The relationship between money and happiness would prove to be a running theme in the field, as two areas of great interest to most Americans intersected.[11]

With broad prosperity in the mid-1920s, both economists and sociologists began to investigate the generally accepted notion that wealthier people were naturally happier than others. Being able to afford not just necessities but the good things in life was understandably assumed to be an ideal basis for happiness, especially in a society that was rapidly embracing mass consumption. Research into the matter, however, was showing that the issue was far more complicated. In his 1925 *The Relation of Wealth to Welfare*, William A. Robson made the case that having a high income did not make one enjoy things any more than someone with a modest income, contradicting classic economic theory. Similarly, a rich person did not enjoy his or her work any more than someone who was not rich, this too inconsistent with what was popularly believed. Much more research had to be done, but it appeared that Americans' tendency to work harder in order to make more money in order to be happier was a faulty proposition.[12]

With plenty of work to be had and plenty of money to be made, however, Americans were determined to rely on our trusted system of consumer capitalism to bring them the happiness they desired and believed they deserved. "America today unquestionably exceeds all other nations in material prosperity," noted T. N. Carver, a Harvard economist, in *Current History* in 1927, the most remarkable thing being that even the working class was able to afford many of the "cheap luxuries" being mass produced. The Machine Age was ushering in a new era defined by greater wealth and more leisure, with no end to the good times in sight. Some critics, especially religious leaders, warned that true happiness was to be found in the enduring values of life rather than in owning new motor cars, radios, and electric appliances, but Americans appeared to be fully enjoying the bountiful marketplace of the late twenties.[13]

The Fine Art of Happiness

The changes taking place along gender lines were also raising questions related to happiness in America. Women of the 1920s were benefitting from the gains made by their older sisters who had led the suffrage movement, and were now pushing the boundaries of gender in a new and, to some, shocking direction. While the suffrage movement was mostly about gaining political freedoms, feminism in the 1920s was grounded in the pursuit of social and economic freedoms, meaning the ability to participate in activities that had been largely limited to men. Women engaged in this pursuit believed that greater social and economic equality would lead to greater happiness, both collectively and individually, but some critics argued something quite different. "Feminism is destructive of women's happiness," Gina Lombroso Ferrero, author of *The Soul of Woman*, plainly put it in 1926, thinking that those seeking all the privileges of men were on a wrong path. Trying to imitate men would backfire on women, she believed, recommending that those of her gender who were seeking greater happiness stay true to their traditional domestic roles.[14]

In a much publicized debate between Corra Harris and Dora Russell (the wife of Bertrand Russell and a recognized intellectual in her own right) set up by *Forum* magazine, Harris went as far as to argue that women of the late 1920s were less happy than their grandmothers had been in Victorian times. While modernity had brought with it a much greater opportunity to not abide by Christian dogma and to get divorced, the costs of such freedoms were high. "There is a greed and ruthlessness in her awful demand for happiness that our grandmothers did not have," the journalist and author wrote in 1928, thinking contemporary women's excessive expectations to be happy ironically made it impossible for them to be so. By being devoted to their families' interests rather than their own, women of the late nineteenth century were happier people, Harris argued, her controversial point of view based on the supposition that the greatest happiness came from caring for others. "No other happiness is like it, because it cannot be diminished or taken away," she concluded, no doubt raising the hackles of feminists convinced that gender equality was the only way that women could be as happy as men.[15]

As one of them, Russell began her "pro-happiness" argument that "the good old days" were not so good for women. The lack of reliable birth control (and abortion options) forced many married women to have children they didn't really want, she pointed out, and wife beating was common. Unmarried women of the day had it even worse, either "eking out miserable existences as poorly paid and dependent governesses" or else having to rely on charity from relatives or benefactors. Far greater independence and self-respect had come to women over the course of the last half-century, Russell stated, their newfound freedoms resulting in a much higher degree of happiness than their grandmothers had enjoyed. In short, there was now the opportunity for women to "give expression to one's own personal needs and desires, to go forward in one's own achievements, and at the same time to cooperate on free and equal terms with other human beings," all of these essential ingredients for human happiness regardless of gender.[16]

As this debate made clear, the shifting plates of gender in the late 1920s were elevating the matter of happiness among women, especially as related to the workplace. More women were taking advantage of the opportunity to pursue careers, raising the question of whether they were more likely to be happy at work or at home, as Ferrero had suggested. Three women debated the subject at a 1929 conference held at New York's Society for Ethical Culture that posed the question, "Does the increasing economic independence of women make for greater happiness?" Each of the speakers presented different answers to the question, illustrating the range of views regarding women's happiness in the modern age. Eleanor Goldmark, who represented unmarried women, defined happiness as "to be alive, experiencing things, and growing," and argued that work outside the home was a logical place for women to find it now that housework was being made so much easier. Mrs. Leo Weill, representing married women, argued that while a mother of young children could find happiness at home, it was often in the best interests of the entire household for women with older or no children to work outside the home as it offered them a "broader outlook" on life. The third panelist, a Mrs. Necarsulmer, however, argued that both unmarried and married women thinking they would realize happiness through the greater economic independence to be found in a career were barking up the wrong tree. Single women would find more happiness in a life guided by spirituality versus materialism, she maintained, and married women pursuing careers would soon discover that "serving two masters" would be a difficult proposition.[17]

Other more conservative observers of the social scene warned women in search of happiness to not take advantage of the new kind of sexual liberties to be had. Lucy Jenkins Franklin, dean of women at Boston University, advised women to not engage in "pre-nuptial petting," claiming that doing so would decrease the chances of a happy marriage. One of the social freedoms feminists of the twenties were striving for was sexual in nature, leading traditionalists like Franklin to find good reasons for women to avoid such temptation. It required "as much study and skill to be a successful wife and mother as it does to be a successful doctor," she told the Society of Harvard Dames in 1926 in a talk titled "Marriage as a Profession," arguing that engaging in premarital sex would work against those planning to find happiness in marriage.[18]

The greater interest in the idea of happiness in America between the world wars had much to do with the spread of psychology-infused thinking in everyday life. The workings of the human mind had become a source of fascination among many Americans, propelling theories regarding the degree of control we had over our emotions, particularly that of happiness. In his 1926 *Understanding Ourselves: The Fine Art of Happiness*, for example, Harold Dearden, a physician, showed how individuals could become happier through an acquaintance with the principles of modern psychology. Since it was the nervous system that regulated both physical and psychical well-being, Dearden maintained in the scientific parlance of the times, one's level of happiness can be managed through inner fortitude and the power of reason. Fears and worries, as well as harmful habits, instincts, impulses, and obsessions, could be eliminated by learning "the fine art of happiness," he argued, with logic and rationalism the means by which to keep the more primitive goings-on of the mind at bay.[19]

Many of those with a scientific background were convinced they held responsibility for bringing greater happiness to people. Science, specifically biology and chemistry, was the basis of life itself, after all, leading professionals in those fields to essentially lay claim to human happiness. In 1927, for example, chemists from all over the world met at Penn State to try to figure out how they could promote science in the United States and, at the same time, demonstrate how it served as an agent for happiness. Chemistry was the heart and soul of industry, the international forum of scientists agreed, something that the general public did not fully recognize or appreciate. Medicine too relied heavily on the kind of work that chemists like them did, with people living longer and healthier lives as a direct result of their efforts. Science deserved much of the credit for the progress of civilization and the happiness that had come with it, these men and women concluded, and it was time to be acknowledged for that.[20]

It was not science but democracy that was most responsible for providing a climate for happiness to flourish among individuals, the more politically inclined argued. Bertrand Russell, the English philosopher (and scientist), made the case that people in democratic countries such as the United States and Great Britain were as a whole not just happier but more intelligent and more progressive than those who lived in more repressive regimes. "If you compare the happiness of the average citizen in your country with the happiness of the average citizen of past times, or of undemocratic countries," he stated in a 1927 debate with the philosopher and historian Will Durant, "it is hardly possible to resist the conclusion that democracy has been a contributing factor in the general distribution of the welfare." While there were obvious advantages to living in a democracy—notably government stability, the opportunity to receive an education, and the ability to receive a fair trial if accused of a crime—Russell would be proved wrong about a half-century later when international surveys revealed that Americans were far from being the happiest people on the planet.[21]

Complete Concord with the Universe

Alongside this school of thought suggesting that personal happiness was primarily a function of external forces such as scientific progress or a democratic form of government was another school that prioritized internal factors. One had to realize a state of harmony involving mind, body, and soul, subscribers to this school believed, sounding a lot like those attracted to New Age philosophy a half-century later. Because happiness could only come from within, adherents to the internal school pointed out, the plethora of recipes offered to individuals seeking greater happiness over the centuries was of little or no help. "All the advice of orators toward the achievement of happiness is wasted energy and wasted words," Rabbi Nathan Krass told congregants at Temple Emanu-El in Manhattan in 1929, confident in his belief that there was no formula to happiness except through one's own devices. "Happy is the man who finds himself in complete concord with the universe and his own nature in a perfectly well body, perfectly balanced mind, and a soul free from evil traits," he continued, convinced that "happiness is not a matter of external circumstances."[22]

Krass's keen insight into the nature of happiness reflected the greater attention being paid to mental health in the United States. Until the late 1920s, happiness was viewed predominantly as a by-product of physical health, something entirely understandable before the advent of both modern psychology and modern medicine. Life was relatively short, after all, and chronic illness common. (The average life span of Americans in 1925 was about sixty years, with the first antibiotic, penicillin, discovered in 1928.) Now, however, with all sorts of psychological theories gaining legitimacy and great advances being made in the medical arena, more recognition was being given to the role of emotions and personality with respect to individuals' happiness. William A. White, then superintendent of St. Elizabeth's Hospital in Washington, D.C., believed mental health to have surpassed physical health as the most important factor in human happiness, telling his psychiatric colleagues exactly that at a 1929 dinner celebrating the twentieth anniversary of the founding of the mental hygiene movement.[23]

Happiness had in fact become a rather popular area of study among a good number of psychologists at the country's leading universities. Personality was being "put under the microscope," as the *New York Times* reported, with professors at Yale, Columbia, and other schools trying to determine which kind of people were happy and why. Goodwin Watson of Columbia, for example, had given a questionnaire to four hundred graduate students at that institution and found that while most of the sample (with an average age of thirty years old) fell somewhere near the middle of the spectrum of happiness, fifty claimed to be extremely happy and another fifty "utterly doleful." A healthy, married man who was popular and outgoing was most likely to be happy, Watson reported, with factors such as intelligence, creativity, race, nationality, religion, athleticism, and financial status playing little or no role.[24] This was the very beginning of dedicated research into happiness in America, with decades to come of polls, surveys, and questionnaires designed to reveal which factors were correlated with the subjective state of being and which were not.

With top scholars now devoting serious study to different aspects of human personality, some were beginning to think of happiness in scientific terms. The publication of Walter A. Pitkin's *The Psychology of Happiness* in 1929 was much anticipated, and not just because the author was a well-respected professor of philosophy and psychology at Columbia. In the book, Pitkin devoted a dozen pages to parsing the personality profile of ex-President Woodrow Wilson, much like how contemporary psychologists have spent considerable time and energy analyzing the mind of President Trump. (Wilson had died five years earlier, so he was an easy target.) Pitkin also delved into the minds of such historical characters as Emily Dickinson, Horace Greeley, Immanuel Kant, Rene Descartes, and Frederic Chopin to determine what made them tick, but it was his analysis of ordinary people that made the book a significant contribution to the study of happiness.[25]

Most important, Pitkin distinguished happiness from related emotions such as pleasure and enjoyment, and argued that achieving the former (and higher) state of being was much more than a matter of luck or chance. By applying scientific principles in the fledging field, he held, a much more complete and accurate portrait of happiness could be developed, one that replaced the folklore and so-called wisdom that had guided the subject for centuries. "He has endeavored to analyze enough personalities to get some light of what happiness consists for different types and so to transfer the study of happiness from the old, deductive basis to the new, scientific, inductive method," Florence Finch Kelly wrote in her review of the book for the *New York Times*. Unhappiness could be cured, Pitkin boldly stated, considering a full awareness of one's traits "the chief decisive factor in happiness."[26]

Some critics, however, were clearly tiring of the mountain of words being devoted to the subject of happiness. "It is a thing to be experienced and not prescribed," V. F. Calverton observed in *The Nation* in 1929 after reading Pitkin's book along with Henri de Man's *Joy in Work*, thinking that such literary missives were a waste of good paper. "Treatment of it in terms of generalizations about what to do to be happy, the happiness of a well-ordered life, or how to live happily, without adequate consideration of the social and economic environment, can be nothing more than the veriest twaddle," Calverton sneered, highly suspect of any and all claims that happiness could be approached scientifically. It was nice to think that people could determine for themselves how happy they wanted to be, but outside forces played a much bigger role in shaping individuals' psychological state than authors believed (or admitted). Besides being misguided, such views were "dangerous," Calverton believed, as they persuaded readers to focus only on their personal happiness and ignore the world around them.[27]

An Indefinable Something

Dangerous or otherwise, the mountain of words being dedicated to happiness showed no sign of shrinking. All sorts of theories were being proposed, with no consensus on how individuals seeking greater happiness should go about it, or even what happiness exactly was. The range of ways by which social observers from different fields were approaching happiness was reason enough for *Forum* magazine to devote some space to trying to define the term itself. As part of its "What is?" series, in which the monthly magazine targeted to more erudite readers invited them to offer their opinions of what a particular term meant, editors dedicated its January 1929 column to the idea of happiness. (Prizes were awarded to those whose submissions were selected for publication.) As with experts in the subject, readers' understanding of the term were all over the map (answers ranged from "an indefinable something" to "a full stomach"), leading the editors to reasonably conclude that "the definition of happiness must vary for each individual and that no single formula can adequately cover it."[28]

What did happiness mean to those readers whose submissions were published? "Happiness is material satisfaction, emotional fulfillment, and spiritual contentment," wrote Alice E. Richeson of St. Louis, obviously seeing it as a fortuitous confluence of various components in life. Mrs. C. T. Marshall of Columbus, Ohio, perceived happiness in more narrow (and Zen-like) terms, defining it as "a state of mind wherein one is at peace with himself and in harmony with his environment." T. A. Williams of Los Angeles, meanwhile, thought happiness could come only if one wasn't worried about what tomorrow might bring, describing it as "a feeling of complete satisfaction with the immediate conditions of life together with a lack of any fear or anxiety to the future." Finally, C. Frederic Marks of Marble Hill, Missouri, viewed happiness though the classically American lens of progress and vitality, defining it as "the attainment of one objective immediately followed by the pursuit of another."[29] Just as with experts on the subject, ordinary Americans appeared to view happiness in very different terms.

The stock market crash in October 1929 and the onset of the Great Depression did little to change the upward trajectory of happiness in America. In his *The Conquest of Happiness* published in 1930, for example, Bertrand Russell again weighed in on the subject, eschewing Pitkin's scientific approach for one based in sociological and philosophical analysis. Despite (still) being the most prosperous people on the planet, he observed, Americans were at the same time the most economically insecure. This would be a theme he would return to in later writings after spending considerable time in the United States as a professor at various universities. Many if not most Americans lived paycheck to paycheck, he noted, and felt trapped in jobs they did not particularly like but had to keep. As well, Americans rode a rollercoaster of happiness based heavily on how well the economy was doing, Russell suggested, this too making individuals feel that they had little control over their own lives.[30] Russell wasn't the only one concluding that a deep strain of unhappiness ran through the United States as a new decade began. "Why are we unhappy?" W. B. Curry asked readers of *The New Republic* in 1930, the question alone suggesting that many Americans were falling well short in their pursuit of happiness.[31]

For Russell, it was Americans' overemphasis on success that posed the biggest obstacle to finding happiness. The price of success was simply too high for most people, he argued, as achieving it required an enormous amount of emotional energy that left little opportunity for individuals to tap into other sources of happiness. Envy too was a major factor in Americans' widespread unhappiness, he believed, our competitive society forcing people to focus on what was missing from their lives rather than what they possessed. Finally, sin played a role in crushing many Americans' chances for realizing happiness, with even those who had come to reject organized religion finding that they still felt guilty or ashamed when committing some act that could be construed as a transgression by their faith.[32]

Russell's acerbic analysis of American-style happiness was typical of those visiting from other countries. Happiness appeared to be a polarized emotion in this country, many a foreigner concluded after spending some time here, contradictory and even paradoxical in nature. "Foreign visitors in the United States either think that Americans are the happiest folk on earth," went a 1931 *New York Times* editorial, "or else find that there is no happiness at all in America." The British writer J. B. Priestley certainly was flummoxed after he returned home, unsure if, as the newspaper reported, "the immense zest with which Americans throw themselves into the pursuit of pleasure does not really mean a desperate attempt to get away from something." Was Americans' penchant to stay busy, regardless of the reason why, an authentic expression of happiness or, conversely, a cover for widespread unhappiness? That Priestley, one of the preeminent social observers between the world wars, couldn't tell revealed how difficult it was not just to recognize happiness but to know how much of it actually existed.[33]

Felix Adler, founder of the Society for Ethical Culture, was more disturbed by what he (and many other religious leaders) considered to be Americans' desperate hunt for happiness. "People of today are too much concerned with thoughts of happiness," he declared in 1931 on the fifty-fifth anniversary of the founding of the humanist organization and congregation, of the opinion that most Americans were blind to the fact that suffering was an essential part of spiritual growth. People now had their sights on achieving happiness rather than pursuing and spreading love, Adler believed, this reorientation from the external to the internal bad for individuals and society as a whole.[34] Harry Emerson Fosdick, pastor at the Riverside Congregation in Manhattan, couldn't have agreed more. "Happiness is not so easy to get at as these individualists think," he told his flock in 1930, thinking that the rampant pursuit of happiness in America was instead resulting in disillusionment and a lack of passion for life.[35]

While Adler thought that Americans' quest for happiness was largely missing the whole point of life, another brilliant mind of the day had a completely different view. "It's happiness we're after," Albert Einstein told an interviewer for a German newspaper in 1931, confessing he didn't care which political system ruled as long as people all over the world were happy. Now that capitalism had failed (it being two years into the Depression), the world-famous scientist continued, he was open to all political alternatives, including some sort of collectivism.[36] Happiness did indeed seem to be on Einstein's big brain. Earlier that same year, he gave a talk entitled "Science and Happiness" at Caltech, questioning whether his field was making the world a better or worse place. "Why does this magnificent applied science which saves work and makes life easier bring us so little happiness?" he asked students, his answer a simple one: "We have not yet learned to make sensible use of it."[37]

A Readjustment of Values

Albert Einstein was hardly the only scientist wondering if people were happier with all the advances made in the past few decades than people in earlier times. The crash and Depression had made many rethink the very notion of progress, and raised the question of whether previous generations were happier because things were simpler. C. E. Kenneth Mees, director of research for Eastman Kodak in Rochester, New York, for example, made headlines when he told a group of colleagues that those who lived in ancient societies thousands of years ago were happier than twentieth-century Americans. "Will any student of history agree that the inhabitants of a American city are, on the whole, happier than those of a Greek or a Babylonian city of the past?" he asked attendees of a symposium (ironically billed as "Engineering Progress") in 1931. Mees said he would be literally happy to have lived thousands of years ago when there was less pressure to both make and spend money, no doubt shocking his fellow engineers with such regressive talk.[38]

Other men of industry, however, remained convinced that progress was a principal instrument of happiness. While our system of consumer capitalism had no doubt experienced a major setback, Charles M. Schwab, chairman of Bethlehem Steel, admitted, good times would soon return as the fundamental law of supply and demand decreed. "I am just as confident as ever that we will ultimately emerge to a period of prosperity and happiness as great if not greater than any we have seen," he told the Pennsylvania Society in 1931, this latest depression a severe one but just part of the normal economic cycle of ups and downs. American happiness was fueled by commerce, businessmen like Schwab believed, and it was commerce that would again serve as its primary agent.[39]

With happiness perceived as a scarce commodity in the early thirties because of economic matters, academics continued to explore the subject in individualistic terms. Randolph C. Sailer, a colleague of Goodwin Watson's at Columbia, had just completed his own psychological test to measure individual happiness, finding that the happiest students (men aged seventeen to thirty-five) were likely to enjoy good health and have a strong faith. Interestingly, it was an even "temper," as it was called at the time, that was most linked to high levels of happiness. Those who maintained an even emotional keel, versus experiencing wide mood swings, were overall the happiest students, a finding that future researchers would uncover in their own studies. Even if one had more ups or highs than downs or lows, in other words, it was better to stay close to equanimity if one desired to be generally happy in life.[40]

Judging by the range of prescriptions for happiness being offered, however, Americans of the early 1930s did indeed appear to be experiencing quite a number of lows. William J. Thompson of Drew University's Theological School in New Jersey felt that the nation's twenty-three million cows enjoyed more tranquility than a similar number of people, a result of Americans failing in their "duty to be happy." Thompson, like many religious leaders, believed unhappiness to be a sin, making it one's responsibility to put happiness over other pursuits in life. Too much focus on work, or more accurately the lack of time being devoted for more spiritual matters, was the cause of widespread unhappiness, he held. Many were indeed working not just weekdays but evenings and weekends, trying to make back the money they had lost in the crash. What then would solve the happiness problem in the United States, according to Thompson? A twenty-five-hour workweek, he proposed, giving people the time that was necessary to realize the "unified inner life" he considered to be the basis for happiness.[41]

Virginia C. Gildersleeve, a dean at Barnard College, argued that it was the misapplication of progressive education that was steering Americans away from a more soulful approach to happiness. Too many teachers were misinterpreting the principles of the pedagogical movement that had begun in the late nineteenth century, she believed, creating a generation of young adults who were reluctant to do anything except what they wanted to do. More individualized, less formal education had seeded false and unrealistic expectations for happiness in society, according to Gildersleeve, but ironically the Depression was making things better in this regard. "What effect are these hard times having on the American pursuit of happiness?" she asked in a 1932 address in St. Paul's Chapel at Columbia, answering that the "one great good coming out of them [was] a readjustment of values." "We are learning that we must re-define happiness in a sterner and far truer sense," Gildersleeve observed, the economic disaster proving to be a much needed reality check.[42]

For those who could still afford it, however, engaging in what would one day be called conspicuous consumption remained a primary way for Americans to find happiness, or at least a reasonable facsimile of it. Edgar J. Goodspeed, who taught Greek at the University of Chicago, was keenly aware that the practice of shopping went far beyond the acquisition of a particular product. In his 1933 *Buying Happiness*, Goodspeed argued that it was the set of emotions that consumers were really purchasing, specifically "pleasure, enjoyment, and happiness." Such thinking, especially from an academic who was best known for his American translation of the New Testament, was quite advanced for the time. Many marketers of the 1930s were sticking to the "hard sell" approach of advertising that relied on facts, logic, and reason to persuade consumers to buy their products. As many marketers today understand, Goodspeed recognized that the material aspects of a product and even its benefits were almost beside the point; it was more the positive feelings that the thing was believed to be capable of creating that consumers really were buying.[43]

As many critics over the years would argue, however, happiness was simply not for sale. Designed to serve individual wants or needs, consumerism was antithetical to the foundation of happiness, according to this line of thought, with only a deep commitment to a worthwhile cause capable of generating the emotion. Others went further to make the case that anyone actively seeking happiness in any way was unlikely to find it, as the state of being was more the result of an other-directed way of thinking or acting. "It comes to us when we are least aware of it, when through some great faith or through some hope for the world to which we give ourselves in honest work we forget ourselves completely," Rabbi Samuel Schulman told his congregation at Temple Emanu-El in

Manhattan in 1933. (Schulman had taken over that pulpit for Rabbi Krass, who had just retired.)[44]

One reporter's visit to Tahiti that year added more support to the idea that an individualized approach to happiness was misdirected. The two hundred members of a leper colony on that island in French Polynesia, of all places, were generally happy people, the journalist found, seemingly more so than the average American. Located in a setting of remarkable beauty, the colony was a self-governed democracy in which each new arrival was given a plot of land on which to build his or her own hut. Everyone was somehow employed, most of them as fishermen or fisherwomen who spent much of their days in boats made by the community. "In the afflicted colony there are no petty jealousies or squabbles," with members committed to "making the lives of the others pleasant," the reporter observed, things the millions of politically divided, economically depressed Americans could only wish for.[45]

Is Everybody Happy?

With moving to an island in the South Seas not in the cards for most, Americans had to look elsewhere to find happiness. There was by the early 1930s no shortage of resources for those interested in acquiring larger quantities of it to consult. Those who knew one best—spouses, relatives, and close friends—might have some useful pointers, while professionals such as clergymen and psychiatrists could possibly serve as fonts of knowledge on the subject. Unfortunately, it was highly unlikely that happiness seekers would gain any useful information from anyone. Some kind of magic formula of happiness was out there waiting to be discovered, many assumed, the hard truth being that no such charm or spell existed. "They cannot grasp the fundamental fact that there is no high-road to happiness," Louis Berg wrote in his 1933 textbook *The Human Personality*, with no "cabbalistic wonders" to be found regardless how hard one tried to find them.[46]

While miraculous revelations of happiness were not forthcoming, Berg did believe that people could follow certain principles that increased one's chances to be happy in life. Pursuing good "mental hygiene" was analogous to pursuing good physical health, he, like many in the medical field at the time, thought, with the former heavily reliant on maintaining a positive attitude and developing what was termed a "balanced" personality. Mental hygiene, the movement founded by Clifford W. Beers in the early twentieth century, combined thinking from many different fields, including medicine, biology, ethics, criminology, sociology, and psychology, leading its proponents to conclude that happiness was largely a result of how individuals related to society. "Social consciousness is the core of adjustment and happiness," Berg stated, with extroverts far more likely to be happy than those who shied away from interaction with others.[47]

Besides loners, single adults were viewed with some suspicion in the domestically oriented 1930s, and were often considered less well adjusted and less happy than those who were married. Happiness was to be found in the security and stability of family life, most experts agreed, a reaction to the uncertainties and anxieties produced by the Depression. Marriage itself was studied closely in order to try to document the factors that went into a successful and happy relationship. Home economists, psychologists, and sociologists paid close attention to which couples were most and least happy, in part to help those who were planning to get married and start families. Gender roles were clearly defined at the time, with a backlash against the freedoms and liberties the modern woman of the 1920s had enjoyed.

The return of more traditional values could certainly be found in a 1934 study completed by the Institute of Family Relations and presented at that year's American Home Economics Convention. Happiness in marriage was largely a function of male domination, Paul Popenoe, director of the organization, told one thousand home economists after hearing the stories of three thousand couples. In short, husbands should be the head of the household, as "wife-ruled" homes were judged to be least happy. Needless to say, it was women who were to blame for unhappy marriages. "The educated wife cannot seem to make up her mind what she wants to be," Popenoe asserted, with such women sometimes wanting to be "the 100 per cent good wife" and other times "the 'new woman' who will submit to nothing."[48]

Some top academics were also examining happiness in marriage, with their findings often used to determine settlements in divorce cases. Ernest Watson Burgess and Leonard S. Cottrell of the University of Chicago were doing work in the field, as was Lewis Madison Terman (known best for his pioneer research in intelligence testing). In 1938, Terman and his team reported the results of a study that examined the relative happiness of eight hundred married couples in California, with findings mirroring what was believed about individual happiness. Income, religion, age, and education were not factors in how happy couples were or weren't, the researchers found, but each spouse's temperament played in a big role in marital happiness ("prenuptial petting" turned out not to be a problem). To Terman's surprise, the happiness of one spouse was largely independent of the other's, hinting perhaps of future research showing that one's genetic profile was a major definer of individual happiness.[49] Two books published that same year—Bell Wiley's *So You're Going to Get Married* and I. M. Hotep's *Love and Happiness*—offered advice to young couples planning to get married, specifically how to find happiness in both sexual relations and domestic situations.[50]

Alongside the greater attention to the pursuit of happiness within marriage and family life was a recasting of the emotion within the public and civic arena. Values rooted in community and nationalism were being celebrated, a backlash against the rampant individualism and materialism of the 1920s that had led to economic disaster. Government officials seized the opportunity to express happiness in collective terms, a means of reassuring Americans that the nation's economic woes would soon be over. "We are headed toward the goal of the greatest happiness for the greatest number of people," Harold L. Ickes, Secretary of the Interior, wrote in 1934, typical communitarian rhetoric of the FDR administration. "We are on our way to raise the standard of living of the great mass of the people, to equalize opportunities and to redistribute wealth fairly and equitably," he continued, further casting happiness as something to be found in the public domain rather than on an individual basis.[51]

The good news for economically minded Americans seeking greater happiness was that by the mid-1930s the worst of the Depression appeared to be over, something President Roosevelt and the First Lady were pleased to tell the American people. There was a "more widespread feeling of happiness" at Christmastime 1934 than the previous year, Eleanor Roosevelt told the media, basing her assessment on the tone of the holiday cards the White House had received.[52] FDR's New Deal was providing many Americans with much-needed work, with even more aggressive federal programs and public works projects to come with the "Second New Deal" that spring. A good number of Republicans were not happy with what could be considered the governmental subsidizing of happiness, seeing such economic relief as inconsistent with the idea that it was up to each individual to produce that desired state of being on his or her own. "More and more people are beginning to think that they will achieve happiness if only they can seize some State largess which they have not had to earn," wrote one such conservative, perceiving the New Deal as altering the evenness of the nation's playing field.[53]

Whether the New Deal was helping the economy or just giving people a free ride, happiness did appear to be in greater abundance than in the darkest days of the Depression. "Is everybody happy?" asked the editors of the *Saturday Evening Post* in 1935, its answer being "Yes! That is, almost everybody." Most farmers were back in business, and consumers had begun to spend money in ways they did before the crash. The stock market was going up and up, and owners of real estate were very happy about the rising value of their investment (partly due to galloping inflation). More than twenty million Americans were on relief, meaning receiving government benefits, and it was this group of people who were perhaps happiest of all given the alternative of starving or freezing to death. "Everybody is happy, except the pessimists here and there," the editors of the magazine observed, with these killjoys not able to ruin the apparent return of happiness in America.[54]

With presumably more opportunity for Americans to pursue happiness now that the economy was getting back on track, a slew of books dedicated to help readers do just that appeared on bookshelves. S. Parkes Cadman's *Adventure for Happiness* (1935), for example, echoed the notion that one had to go out and grab happiness rather than wait for it to come to you. "It can not be too often asserted that happiness is a state of mind secured by one's own endeavor," the well-known clergyman and author wrote, stating that "sagacious as well as strenuous effort" was required to acquire the genuine version of it.[55] Boris Sokoloff's *The Achievement of Happiness,* published that same year, argued that people were naturally "wired" to be happy, but individuals had to overcome physical and mental obstacles to reach the state. While the Russian physician had much to say about the role of glands in human happiness, it was love, he believed, that served as its guiding principle.[56] John Cowper Powys's *The Art of Happiness* (also 1935), meanwhile, traced how the author had found his happiness and how readers could follow the same formula. "Project your soul from your troubled brain, or pretend to yourself that you project it," went one of his mental tricks, convinced that one could fool oneself into being happy.[57]

That was indeed quite the year (1935) for what was fast becoming a recognizable literary genre dedicated to happiness. Charles Francis Potter's *Technique of Happiness* preferred to think of happiness as "applied hedonics," the science of which remained largely not understood. Individuals tossed dozens of variables into their personal bucket of happiness, he believed, accounting for why achieving it (as well as studying it) was so complicated and challenging. The fact that each person had his or her own unique set of variables made study of the subject that much more difficult, he added. Still, it was incumbent upon people to determine the precise sources of their unhappiness and then find ways to convert them to happiness, this the technique promised in the book's title. For most readers, however, it's safe to say that Potter's "simple" technique of happiness, as he described it, was much easier said than done.[58]

The Most Elusive of Human Goods

While the abundant literature being produced shed some light on the subject of happiness and no doubt helped some readers find it, it was clear that the field, if there even was one, was still in its infancy. The pursuit of happiness was central to the lives of most people, yet the subject resided on the margins of both science and the humanities. Serious study of happiness was largely limited to a few professors at Columbia, and the numerous books being written about it each came at the subject in its own way, making the area a scattered and muddled one. Observing this, an editor for the *New York Times* posed these very good questions to readers:

> If happiness is so important, why is it not at least made the subject of special courses of study? Why are there not professors of happiness and college classes in elementary and advanced happiness, and happiness research institutes? Why do most intellectuals consider it somewhat naïve to write or to read books on how to be happy? And why has so little progress been made in the subject—why is the latest book on it so much like the first?[59]

It was true that despite the different angles authors were taking, happiness literature tended to blur together and leave one with the feeling that one didn't know much more about the subject than before picking up a book or two or three about it. "The greatest writers, when they talk of happiness, seem somehow able to turn out only platitudes," the editor continued, "truths more neatly put than before, perhaps, but still truths that our grandfathers and great-grandfathers had heard before." It was true that as yet there was precious little original or fresh thinking on the subject, with the same old bromides put forth in new packaging. Happiness was fleeting, we were repeatedly told, and chasing it rarely offered the chance to actually catch it. Leisure and pleasure were not the same as happiness, standard thinking on the subject also made clear, with only hard, purposeful work of some kind able to lead to the latter. "With all the wisdom that has been uttered about it, happiness remains the most elusive of human goods," the *Times* editor concluded, of the mind that "an impenetrable veil hangs over the secret of getting as much of it as we should like."[60]

Such keen observations did nothing to prevent more great minds from uttering more wisdom on the subject of happiness. Marjorie Barstow Greenbie's 1936 *In Quest of Contentment* refreshingly avoided the inspirational, overly optimistic tone of most books about happiness, and made no claim that achieving the state of being was a simple process. In fact, Greenbie made the all-too-rare case that there was little reason for most Americans to be happy given the complexity of everyday life in the 1930s. As others had argued, it was easier for people in earlier "less civilized" times to find happiness, she suggested, with modernity bringing with it not just scientific and technological wonders but considerable confusion and anxiety. "Most of us manage with great success to be miserable," she wrote, with three things—health issues, lack of love, and never having enough money—the cause of widespread discontent. In addition, there was a "general sense of insufficiency in life," Greenbie believed, with, again, only mental discipline and self-determination able to overcome this nagging feeling of dissatisfaction.[61]

Charles Gray Shaw's *The Road to Happiness*, published the following year, instead argued that there was much happiness in modern life, but one needed to know where to look for it. "Human happiness is not to be experienced in some extraordinary state of existence, as on a picnic or in paradise, but is found everywhere in everyday life as color abounds in nature," the professor of philosophy wrote in the book, considering its successful discovery to be mostly a matter of perspective and attitude. More so than other authorities on the subject, Shaw recognized that contemporary American happiness was different from that of other societies and from that of the past. Rather than perceive happiness through a lens of beauty or order (as the ancient Greeks did), for example, Americans viewed it in terms of achievement and accomplishment, a key, often overlooked, distinction. Shaw's "road to happiness" thus lay in the ability to triumph over the many obstacles that faced Americans in the twentieth century, an interesting take on the subject that was entirely consistent with the nation's core values.[62]

For William Moulton Marston, who had led Harvard's psychological laboratory before becoming a consultant in the field, happiness was a function of three Ls: living, loving, and laughing. Marston, who was also credited with having invented the lie detector test, rejected what could be called the "inspirationalist" approach to happiness, in which individuals were advised to direct as much energy as possible to be successful in life. Simply doing what one enjoyed most would lead to both success and happiness, he told fellow members of the Harvard Club in 1937, citing six famous Americans—Henry Ford, Margaret Sanger, FDR, Thomas E. Dewey, the actress Helen Hayes, and Mayor Fiorello LaGuardia—as people who had done just that.[63]

While living, loving, and laughing was as good a recipe for happiness as any, it was evident that most Americans were not doing enough of any or all of them as the 1930s would wind down. Another world war had begun in Europe, and many believed that the United States would have to enter it at some point. The nation's economy had more than recovered from the Great Depression, but more money in Americans' pockets was not leading to greater happiness. One sign that happiness in America was as elusive as ever could be found in the attendance numbers of the free evening classes offered by St. John's University in Brooklyn. The university offered twenty-four weekly courses in all kinds of subjects, including business, politics, and sociology, but the most popular was the one titled "Psychology and Happiness." Four hundred fifty students from New York City, New Jersey, Long Island, and Westchester were crowding into the classroom for the class, with 411 enrolled in the second most popular one, called "Psychology and Marriage." The world was on the brink of crisis, but it was personal happiness that remained on the minds of many Americans.[64]

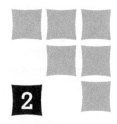

THE PARADOX OF
HAPPINESS, 1940–1959

Happiness presupposes freedom from fear and want,
freedom from anxiety. —Martin Gumpert, 1946

I n December 1945, *Scholastic Magazine* polled one hundred thousand high school students across the country to learn what young people wanted out of life. The Second World War had ended just a few months earlier, so it was an opportune time for the publisher to know more about the goals and aspirations of American teenagers as they looked to their future. The findings revealed that high schoolers appeared to know much more about the dynamics of happiness than their parents, who planned to get on the postwar fast track as soon as possible in order to reap the long awaited consumerist rewards of the Allied victory. Forty-four percent of the teens desired "to live a simple but secure and happy life without making a lot of money or becoming famous," *Scholastic* reported, eleven times more than the 4 percent who sought to get rich. "Only those who are happy can be really successful in life," one student explained, another saying that "people could be a lot happier if they weren't trying to be 'big shots' all the time." A good number of the young people also seemed to recognize that a good route to personal happiness would be serving society in some way. "When I sit down and think about happy and secure people, they are those that have done something for the community," one stated, an insight that many adults had yet to discover in their own chase for happiness.[1]

The interest in what young people wanted out of life as they looked to the future reflected the fact that all Americans' pursuit for happiness had been largely suspended during the war. Broad prosperity would return by midcentury, however, again raising expectations among many to realize that much desired emotional state. Happiness was an essential component of the nation's two core mythologies, the American Dream and the American Way of Life, after all, and a fundamental way we were different from (and considered superior to) the grim Russians and the robotic Chinese. As the 1950s rolled on, however, it would become clear that the competitive nature of capitalism and the pressure to conform to social norms were preventing Americans from finding happiness rather than enabling them to find it. As well, popular culture of the time, notably the genres of film noir, science fiction, and melodrama, suggested that there was a darker side to American life that had little or nothing to do with happiness. Cold War tensions, anticommunist paranoia, and the possibility that the world could blow up any moment were obviously in direct contradiction to the superficial aura of happiness that pervaded American society that decade. The postwar years illustrated "the paradox of happiness," as *Catholic World* put it in 1953, with the gap between the promise and the reality of happiness arguably never wider.[2]

New Goals of Happiness

While happiness could obviously be found during wartime (well-paying jobs were plentiful, even for women, and all kinds of products could be sourced in a thriving black market if one knew whom to ask), homefront Americans were not encouraged to display too much pleasure while others were fighting bravely and dying overseas. Tight restrictions on consumer goods had made the legitimate marketplace considerably less bountiful, another reason for happiness to be sharply curtailed until peacetime. Until then, experts advised Americans to be content by enjoying simple things, and keep their expectations of happiness to a minimum. "For happiness, take a step down," wrote a journalist in *Good Housekeeping* in 1943, recommending that readers on the homefront limit their pleasures to those found in daily life as long as the war waged overseas.[3]

More than anything else, however, happiness during the war years was framed as something to be experienced by Americans in the future after victory was achieved. "After this war is won," President Roosevelt plainly put it in his 1944 State of the Union message, "we must be prepared to move forward . . . to new goals of happiness and well-being."[4] The futuristic orientation of happiness was already apparent as it became evident that the country would likely have to enter the war at some point. That happiness in America was essentially on hold could be detected in October 1940, when twelve hundred people attended a fancy dinner at the Hotel Astor in New York to raise money for the United Hospital Fund. The slogan of that year's campaign was "For Future Happiness," a reference that the funds raised would be used to provide hospital services to the less fortunate during and especially after the war. Each attendee was asked to donate the equivalent of what it would cost to kill thirty of the enemy, oddly enough, a disturbing but certainly compelling means of getting the fat cats to pull out their wallets.[5]

Casting Americans' concept of happiness against that of Nazis was also important to rally a divided citizenship around the war effort. Hitler's goal was to bring happiness not just to Germany but to the world, according to Nazi rhetoric, an idea that no doubt persuaded some isolationists to reconsider their position. The Fuhrer's "God-given natural mission" was to make the world "happy and reasonable," announced Robert Ley, head of the German Labor Front, making it clear that Hitler planned to export his racist and anti-Semitic philosophy when the Nazis won the war. A "better, happier future" lay ahead with the defeat of liberal democracy and Western-style capitalism, Ley predicted, with the Third Reich's politics of national socialism to serve as the basis for widespread happiness by restoring order to the world.[6]

With the entry of the United States into the war after Pearl Harbor, Americans' search for happiness took a back seat to doing what one could to help the Allied Forces achieve victory. By late 1944, when it seemed all but certain that the war would soon be over, happiness in America began to reemerge from the shell it had been in for the last five or so years. However, readjusting back to a peacetime economy would not be easy, many experts believed, with broad happiness heavily dependent on how smoothly that process went. "It is no exaggeration to say that the happiness of every American for the next two generations depends on the efforts and understanding of all of us in this gigantic job of readjustment," warned a general in the armed forces in November of that year, particularly worried about conflict between management and unions as government contracts were terminated. "Jobs and money in the bank" would be the keys to happiness in America for decades to come, the general believed, he like many others already looking forward to the economic windfall and consumer abundance of the postwar years.[7]

Largely neglected during the Depression and World War II due to more pressing matters, Americans' pursuit of happiness became a major discussion point in the national conversation in the late 1940s. After enduring a decade and a half of thrift and sacrifice and being pressured to put the communal good over individual interests, Americans were now primed to realize their own versions of happiness. Happiness was deeply embedded in the American Way of Life centered around the free-market capitalism that so many had fought and died for, and perceived as one of the natural outcomes of our democratic principles. Despite glaring discrimination along racial and gender lines, the postwar years would offer an unprecedented opportunity for most citizens to achieve happiness, popular thought went at the time, with economic prosperity and international harmony to guide the way. As well, advances made during the war helped to spark what can be considered the beginnings of the science of happiness. Combined with further strides in psychology and specifically mental health (and illness), researchers began to explore the whats, whys, and hows of happiness. What is happiness, anyway? these relatively early neuroscientists wondered, seeking a deeper understanding of what was a cognitively murky concept. Up to this time, happiness had been considered something one had complete control over, but that was starting to change with serious enquiry into the emotional workings of the human brain.

The elevation of happiness to nearly religious proportions after the war belied the fact that no one still really knew how to define or measure that state of being. As a discussion among scholars at an August 1945 conference at Columbia University plainly revealed, some of the most brilliant minds of the day struggled to come to terms with the concept of happiness while acknowledging that it would play a key role in the lives of individuals in the years ahead. Just a couple of weeks after the surrender of Japan, 130 academics from a variety of disciplines attempted to determine what kind of common ground would be required in order for people all over the world to be happy. While the professors agreed that the use of atomic weapons forever altered the very nature of existence, none of them could articulate what cultural bridges would have to be formed to serve as a basis for global happiness. It may have been the beginning of a new era in human history, but it was clear that happiness, both its pursuit and the term itself, was as nebulous as ever.[8]

The way that one defined happiness often had much to do with one's profession. Martin Gumpert, a New York City physician and author of *You Are Younger than You Think*, had an unusually clear vision of happiness based on what he did for a living. "Happiness is a medical problem," he declared in *The Nation* in 1946, firmly believing that not just biology had a lot to do with it but that the practice of medicine had a social purpose to promote the state of being through its dedication to physical and mental health. "It is the physician's task—and the basis of his professional dignity and social standing—to achieve and to protect health and thereby create happiness," he wrote, advising his colleagues to be continually on the lookout for signs of unhappiness among their patients. Most physicians at the time (and many today) were interested only in problems of the body, leaving the emotional side of things to their psychiatric colleagues. Early studies in the area were showing that there was a connection between the health of the body and mind, however, something Gumpert appeared to know based on his own experience. Gumpert envisioned a new field of "medical sociology," which he defined as "a systematic effort by physicians to analyze the social causes of unhappiness which influence the health of their patients." The doctor was forward-thinking in not only linking happiness to physical health but by recognizing that social and cultural factors played an important role in shaping the psychological well-being of individuals.[9]

One did not have to be a physician or possess a PhD to reach the conclusion that a democratic society offered a greater chance than other political systems for individuals to be happy. Nazis and Fascists were simply less happy people than those living in a democracy, David

Baumgardt, a philosopher at the Library of Congress who attended the Columbia conference, maintained, a view supported by a group of junior high school students taking part in a 1947 Youth Forum sponsored by the *New York Times*. Because the government in a democracy was made up of and worked for the people, the six New York City–area students taking part in the panel discussion agreed, it was much better suited to facilitate citizens' happiness than dictatorships or totalitarian states. In fact, one of the main goals of a democracy was to help people attain happiness, the students held, something quite different than the political structures of not just our wartime enemies but that of communists as well.[10] Contrasting our democratic way of life to that of communists was becoming a common activity among Americans young and old, with our constitutionally declared freedom to pursue happiness a useful device to do just that.

It's in Your Power

Alongside the macro view of happiness that prevailed in the late forties (i.e., that political systems functioned as an overarching framework that either enabled or limited citizens to pursue those things likely to make them happy), more attention was beginning to be paid to how individuals could expedite the process on their own. Although what would be called self-help books could certainly be found in the 1930s—notably Walter Pittman's *Life Begins at 40* and Dorothea Brande's *Wake Up and Live*, each a bestseller—it wasn't until the late 1940s when the category could be considered a legitimate literary genre. Finding greater happiness was a key component of midcentury thought dedicated to self-improvement, perhaps because many people's expectations regarding that state of being exceeded what they were actually experiencing. "Both the bookstores and magazine-stands are well loaded these days with material which by exhortation, inspiration or information purports to help the reader make a better man of himself," Harry M. Davis observed in the *New York Times* in 1947, adding that this body of work had little to do with the also flourishing psychoanalytic branch of mental health. The peace had been won and there were plenty of well-paying jobs to be had, so why wasn't I happy? a good number of Americans were asking themselves a couple of years after the war, with the answer not at all clear.[11]

A good example of early postwar self-help oriented toward happiness was Roger F. Lapham's *It's in Your Power* published that same year. Like Gumpert, Lapham was a physician and similarly merged the realization of happiness with good health, seeing emotional and physical well-being as two sides of the same coin. Fears and worries led not just to unhappiness but poor health, he had found in his practice, with many of his patients using alcohol to try to make their problems go away. Rather than regret what took place in the past and be anxious about what might happen in the future, Lapham advised, confronting current and real challenges head on was the best means of achieving a healthy body and mind. With its focus on self-determination and personal autonomy, *It's in Your Power* anticipated later self-help thought that argued that being happy was a choice that individuals could make.[12]

Some found it not surprising that, given our lack of training in human relationships, many if not most Americans were not particularly happy people. Happiness relied heavily on the ability to live and work with others, psychologists and sociologists agreed, yet there was no formal opportunity for individuals to learn how to do that. Such was the case made by Leonard S. Cottrell Jr., a sociologist at Cornell University, urging that courses in human relations become part of college curricula in the country to raise our individual and collective happiness quotient. Conflict of one kind or another was a natural part of personal and professional relationships, he observed, making it strange that we were not taught how to resolve clashes or provided with techniques that could be useful in this regard. The divorce rate was rising rapidly after the war, leading Cottrell, who specialized in marriage and family, to think that a general inability to amiably work out disagreements had much to do with domestic discord. Much was being made about the inalienable rights and freedoms of the individual to pursue happiness, he noted, but it was largely overlooked that virtually all of this activity took place in social or group settings in which differences of opinion were likely to occur.[13]

Another leading sociologist of the day, William F. Ogburn, viewed not a lack of proficiency in relationships but the rise of larger, more complex, and more powerful organizations as the biggest threat to Americans' happiness. Bureaucracy was indeed increasing in both government and industry at midcentury, posing a threat to both the idea and practice of democracy in the nation. We had fought the latest war (as well as the Revolutionary War) in part in opposition to all-encompassing power of the state or any other institution, but it was now clear that centralized authority was on the rise in both the political and economic arenas. There was indeed a growing intolerance for challenging the status quo, reflected by the very real risks involved with opposing the ideological principles of the consensus. Achieving one's personal version of happiness was contingent on the ability for individuals to chart their own course, according to our national ethos, good reason for Ogburn to be worried that we could be heading into dangerous waters.[14]

Sensing that tension, perhaps, the editors of *Life* magazine brought together eighteen prominent men and women in 1948 to discuss Americans' pursuit of happiness. Over a weekend at the Westchester Country Club in Rye, New York, the dozen and a half handpicked notables from business, academia, publishing, religion, and the arts "reinterpreted in modern terms a great Jeffersonian right," as the magazine told readers in its report of the discussion. How had the "pursuit of happiness" changed since it was conceived 172 years ago? the editors wondered, and was it even still relevant? Was the current pursuit of happiness helping society in some way, or was it purely self-oriented? If anyone could answer such tough questions, it was these experts believed to have special insight into the American character near midcentury. Russell W. Davenport, who had been managing editor of *Fortune* and worked for Wendell Willkie during his 1940 presidential campaign, served as moderator for the summit.[15]

First and foremost, Davenport asked the group, were contemporary Americans succeeding in their inalienable right to be happy? Even these esteemed experts (who included Henry Luce, editor in chief of *Life, Time,* and *Fortune* magazines) weren't sure, taking the findings of national surveys with a large grain of salt. *Ladies' Home Journal* had recently completed a poll that showed that a whopping 91 percent of Americans described themselves as either "very" or "fairly" happy, for example, but more qualitative evidence suggested otherwise. A high divorce rate, rising juvenile delinquency and crime, and a record number of "psycho-neurotic" cases were just a few signs that all was not well in the country. As well, many Americans were using alcohol in quantities that went far beyond reasonable social lubrication, another sign that there might be trouble in paradise (annual consumer spending on liquor was three times the nation's budget for education). Erich

Fromm, the eminent psychoanalyst whose new book, *Man For Himself*, was selling briskly, pointed out that the gap between self-perception and reality was typically a large one, explaining why surveys designed to measure individuals' happiness were of little value. All in all, the group felt that there was "a failure in America to achieve genuine happiness," Davenport wrote in his report, quite a conclusion given that all the participants had made it to the top of their respective field. Exposing the cracks in the postwar American Way of Life was a brave thing for Luce to do, especially in his magazine, which was viewed around the world as a leading voice of the country itself.[16]

Why exactly were many if not most Americans less than happy despite what they told pollsters? "The modern individual is out of touch with the inner realities of life and is somehow 'lost,'" Davenport proposed based on the group's discussion, with general agreement that the average American suffered from "philosophical and spiritual confusions." The philosophy professors and religious leaders who had been invited to the weekend especially felt that way, seeing a lack of values in contemporary life that gave citizens little or no moral and ethical structure. "What is missing is a philosophy of the whole man," remarked Father Edmund A. Walsh of Georgetown University, thinking the problem of happiness was a function of some kind of a deficiency in Americans' inner selves.[17]

Interestingly, other attendees at *Life*'s roundtable felt that Americans' struggle to find happiness was not an inner problem but an outer one. It was the "system" that was preventing individuals from realizing genuine happiness, some argued, specifically that our social and economic institutions were in conflict with emotional well-being. Work had for the most part become dull and monotonous in the Machine Age, panelists agreed, and leisure—particularly the movies—was more an exercise in escapism than anything else (television was of course in the process of becoming a prime source of entertainment that further lowered the bar of the arts, according to the intellectual elite). Advertising raised material expectations to an unhealthy degree, attendees also concurred, and gave the false impression that happiness was, in Fromm's words, "a commodity one can buy." It was Stuart Chase, an author and sociologist, however, who perhaps most succinctly captured Americans' challenge finding happiness. It was impossible for any intelligent person to be completely happy under the constant threat of nuclear apocalypse, he believed, thinking that the possibility of World War III breaking out anytime put a damper on both individual and collective happiness in the United States.[18]

The Greatest Achievement
of Any Human Being

Life magazine's refreshingly candid report on the state of happiness in the United States at midcentury did not discourage Americans from trying to become happier people. In fact, now that the economy was on citizens' side, many shifted their pursuit into a higher gear, pressured by the fact that others appeared to be getting ahead of them in the race for success. As in the 1930s, there were plenty of happiness how-tos targeted to readers feeling a little help couldn't hurt. In 1950, for example, *Woman's Home Companion* offered readers a "ten-day plan for happiness," reducing what Fromm believed was "the greatest achievement of any human being" into a relatively quick and easy exercise in self-improvement.[19] Articles offering advice to readers looking for greater happiness in their lives often appeared in women's magazines during these and the following years, suggesting that many American housewives were finding domestic life unfulfilling on some level. In September 1946, for example, *Ladies' Home Journal* addressed the question "What Makes People Happy?" with *Vogue* a decade later showing readers how to have a "Happy Heart."[20] In 1957, *Better Homes & Gardens* informed readers that "Happiness Is Where You Are," addressing women seemingly wondering if greater happiness could be found doing something else somewhere else.[21]

Secular religion also not infrequently informed happiness self-help in the postwar years. Such was the case in Norman Vincent Peale's and the aptly named Smiley Blanton's 1950 *The Art of Real Happiness*, in which Bible verse made regular appearances. The authors made no attempt to separate religion from happiness, in fact, describing their purpose as to help readers gain "joy, contentment, security, and a stronger faith to meet the adversities of life." There was a long-running feud between psychologists and the clergy, but no such division could be detected in this book.[22] Other books such as James Gordan Gilkey's *Here Is Help for You* (1951) and Peale's hugely popular *The Power of Positive Thinking* (1952) were considered valuable resources for those whose level of personal happiness was less than what society was telling them it should be.[23] Ways to ride out tough patches in a marriage was a subsegment of postwar happiness how-tos, as was advice on avoiding getting caught up in the competitive spirit of the times.

Although there was no shortage of literary resources designed to help readers find their own version of happiness, serious study of the subject was in short supply. Lin Yutang observed as much for *Saturday Review* in 1950, asking the question "Do American writers shun happiness?" Yutang, the well-known, Chinese-born writer who had just published *On the Wisdom of America*, was surprised that many of the deepest thinkers in this country had overlooked or consciously avoided happiness in their writings, feeling perhaps that its intangibility and tenuousness were too much for even them to take on. "Common sense tells us that happiness is what everybody is striving for and yet with all the past and present wisdom of men no one has attempted to tell us how to get there," he wrote, dismissing all the how-tos as silly bonbons that offered readers little or no real insight into the difficult process. It was true that who Yutang considered the "wittiest and wisest Americans minds," including Emerson, Twain, Will Rogers, William James, John Dewey, and Tom Paine, had not weighed in on the subject, at least with the intellectual rigor that it demanded. Thoreau was the possible exception, but "he went too far," from Yutang's point of view, the latter thinking there was much more to life to be enjoyed than communing with nature by oneself.[24]

It was true that, despite its centrality to the human and especially American experience, happiness was not the focus of any discipline, field, or general approach to life. Philosophers were primarily interested in the concept of truth, Yutang pointed out, while devout Christians were more concerned with finding salvation than happiness. Capitalists were dedicated to accumulating wealth rather than the range of emotions it could possibly offer, and socialists prioritized the collective good over individual happiness. Even hedonists, who one might think would be fully invested in the subject, were actually keener on experiencing pleasure than achieving happiness. What was it about happiness that made anyone and everyone veer away from it instead of confronting it head-on? "It would be wonderful if there existed a philosophy devoted entirely to a study of the aims, methods, and possibilities of attaining happiness in this present life," Yutang noted, not knowing of course that something much like that would take shape in another couple of decades.[25]

Fromm's 1955 *The Sane Society* clearly showed that some present-day writers were willing to tread into the choppy waters of happiness. As he had at *Life*'s weekend retreat in Rye some years back, Fromm (who had emigrated to the United States in 1934) thoughtfully parsed the meaning of happiness in contemporary America, arguing that our consumerist society was encouraging individuals to look to materialism to find it rather than inside themselves. "Happiness is a state of intense inner activity and the experience of the increasing vital energy which occurs in productive relatedness to the world and to ourselves," he wrote, powerful words that implied it could not be acquired on a lay-away plan like a new Frigidaire or Studebaker. While a desire for the good things in life was not inherently a bad thing, he believed, the tail was now wagging the dog with regard to consumerism in Western culture. "Consumption was a means to an end, that of happiness," he noted, but, by the middle of the twentieth century, it "has become an aim in itself."[26]

Others with a deep understanding of the complexity of happiness scoffed at the ways in which the emotional state was being packaged like soap. In 1952, for example, Simeon Stylites could not resist writing a letter to the *Christian Century* after reading a brief Associated Press article (originally published in the *New York Times*) with the headline "Happiness of Public Put Squarely Up to Business." With another war raging, this time in Korea, global politics were as complicated as ever, but American businesses were seemingly up to the task of making Americans happy people. "At least one great problem which has baffled the human race for ten thousand years will soon be definitely settled," Stylites wrote satirically, finding it amusing that it would be business executives, rather than "poets, philosophers, prophets, and preachers," who would crack the code of happiness. It was specifically Jervis J. Babb, president of Lever Brothers, who was responsible for solving the conundrum, telling a thousand members of the Harvard Business School Association that "the nation's business must be responsible for leading people to greater happiness." Happiness could be found in consumption, Babb was saying, and it was up to the men and women of industry to make it all possible. "Let's go shopping and be happy," Stylites jested, urging readers of his letter to get "all aboard for happiness!"[27]

Happiness was often woven into popular culture of the 1950s, of course, reinforcing the idea that it was a desirable and perhaps expected state of being. Popular television shows like *I Love Lucy*, *Make Room for Daddy*, and *Father Knows Best* suggested that both happiness and success were waiting for those who conformed to what a postwar family should look and act like. Fictionalized happiness could be found in abundance on *Cavalcade of America*, a radio program that moved to television in 1953. Week in and week out, the lead character, almost always a man, would fight all odds to achieve something great and find a place in history. A brave and beautiful woman was inevitably at his side, convincing her driven but self-doubting man to keep at it just when he felt all hope was lost. Eventually, of course, the man would make his great discovery, invent some lifesaving drug, or become president, these weekly success stories serving as dramatic tutorials in American-style happiness.[28]

One of the paradoxes of happiness during the postwar years was that the search to find it appeared to be intensifying despite an ever-growing amount of advice dedicated to it. One would think that people would need less advice as they took what was available at the time and presumably became happier, but this simply wasn't the case. There seemed to be an unlimited demand for guidance regarding happiness, with no single piece of wisdom or even the aggregate able to satisfy Americans' craving for contentment and peace of mind. No shortage of formulae for happiness could be found in midcentury America, with people from all walks of life ready to put forth their prescription in hopes they would be recognized as experts in the field.

The idea of happiness often found its way into commencement exercises at all levels of the educational spectrum. How young people could find happiness in their lives as they graduated was (and remains) a go-to oratory platform for speechmakers, as successful individuals offered their thoughts on the matter based on their experience. In 1951, for example, John D. Rockefeller III gave a talk at the commencement exercises at Children's Village in Dobbs Ferry, New York, choosing happiness as his theme. For a century, Children's Village had served as a school for underprivileged or "maladjusted" boys, even more reason why the forty-five-year-old philanthropist and heir to a fortune believed his personal take on happiness would be well received. "The road to happiness lies in two simple principles," Rockefeller told the one hundred boys in attendance, the first being to "find what it is that interests you and that you do well" and the second being to then "put your whole soul into it, every bit of energy and ambition and natural ability you have." Rockefeller's expertise was giving his father's money away, but his principles were every bit as good as some of the most popular self-improvement advice of the day.[29]

Happiness was also a common theme in sermons delivered in houses of worship. Religious leaders often sought to divert worshipers' inclination to find happiness in more corporeal settings, stressing that a higher state of bliss could be found in faith. As familiar as anyone is with the human condition, however, people of the cloth were capable of offering other, impressive insight into the workings of happiness. In 1952, for example, the Reverend John Sutherland Bonnell, pastor of the Fifth Avenue Presbyterian Church in Manhattan, offered his thoughts on happiness that went far beyond following the Ten Commandments. "Whoever heard of anyone finding happiness by chasing it?" the reverend asked his flock, suggesting that making the desire to be happy the central purpose of one's life would prove to be a futile effort. Happiness could not be created but rather happened to those who put themselves in service to others, he pointed out, something that took many people a lifetime to figure out. "Those who bring sunshine into the lives of others cannot keep it from themselves," Bonnell preached, considering the seeking of pleasure "an outmoded technique" in realizing happiness.[30]

The Harmony within You

Happiness advice targeted at women could be considered a category all its own in the early 1950s. We look back on the roles of women during the postwar era as extremely limited, and rightly so given the leaps made a generation later, but the fact was that there was much concern at the time regarding how "modern" women were disrupting life both at home and in the workplace. Many women had by then excelled in college and/or had attained professional positions, causing considerable alarm to traditionalists thinking such strides signaled the end of the American family and the American male as we knew each. More conservative types even considered the mass consumerization of such appliances as the washing machine and vacuum cleaner as a worrying development that made one wonder what women would do with all their time now that housework had become so (supposedly) simple.[31]

Given such thinking, it was not surprising that such "modern" women faced (or at least were believed to face) a significant challenge in finding happiness. Then as now, striking a balance between one's family and work lives was not an easy thing to do, leading some in the happiness field to make that their area of expertise. Working women typically remained in charge of household duties and raising children, putting significant pressure on them to decide how to best divide their time and energy. Many women who left their prestigious jobs to take care of the house and kids found themselves bored, this too why books like Sidonie M. Gruenberg's and Hilda Sidney Grech's 1952 *The Many Lives of Modern Woman: A Guide to Happiness in Her Complex Role* proved popular. "It offers comfort to the depressed young Phi Beta Kappa who finds herself engaged in a daily struggle with diapers and dishes," Jane Cobb wrote of the book in her review for the *New York Times*, thinking women's happiness was "a serious situation [that] deserves serious attention."[32]

Indeed it was, given how many American men (and women), some of them seemingly intelligent, were saying that a woman could find happiness only in the home. Sloan Wilson, who had published his best-seller *The Man in the Gray Flannel Suit* in 1955, for example, made it known that he believed that mothers in gray flannel suits (or their fashion equivalent) was a bad idea. Bernice Fitz-Gibbon, who headed up her own advertising agency in the 1950s, took on Wilson, arguing that not just mothers but both their husbands and children would be "far, far happier if mama is in town carving out a career for herself." Women in the workplace was hardly a new phenomenon, Fitz-Gibbon (who had attended *Life*'s weekend retreat when she was head of advertising at Gimbel's, the department store) correctly pointed out, something men had no problem with when their jobs were largely limited to domestics, servants, teachers, nurses, or secretaries. "It is only since some of the girls began to climb out of the Hoover aprons and into the Chanel and Dior suits and onto the five-figure payroll and into the corner office with the broadloomed floor that the boys have gone in for headshakings and mutterings and hues and cries and anguished plaints (like Sloan Wilson's) about woman's place being in the home," she wrote in 1956, her experience showing that women "can best achieve happiness with homes, children—and jobs."[33]

The impact of modernism upon happiness was also the subject of R. M. MacIver's 1955 *The Pursuit of Happiness: A Philosophy for Modern Living*. For both women and men, MacIver argued, modern life impeded the finding of happiness in that it prioritized materialism over self-awareness, the latter essential to gaining peace of mind. Modernity had also allowed us to devote more time to leisure, he suggested, but this too discouraged happiness by steering us away from the contemplation of the self. For MacIver, who had written and taught for decades in the areas of political science and sociology at Columbia University, happiness relied on the ability to detach oneself from other people and social activities, a difficult thing to do in these days of intense peer pressure and conformity.[34]

Like Fromm's *The Sane Society* published that same year, MacIver's *The Pursuit of Happiness* obviously went much deeper than the quasi-psychology being offered in the sea of how-tos. Although he was an academic, it was clear that the seventy-three-year-old MacIver knew considerably more about how individuals could find greater happiness than did all the self-improvement experts combined. Americans too often lived in the past and future, he argued in the book, with only living in the "momentary now" leading to the type of happiness so many were seeking. Anticipating the kind of thinking in the field that was a few decades away, notably the concept of "flow," MacIver recognized that time tended to stand still or disappear when one was truly happy, with only the present able to offer that level of transcendence. Equally impressive, he was keenly aware of the individualization of happiness (i.e., that it was a different experience for everyone), this too making him ahead of his time. "Happiness is the resonance of the whole being as it moves towards that which fulfills it," MacIver poetically wrote, nicely boiling down the abstract concept into "the harmony within you."[35]

The closer examination of happiness in the United States in the 1950s, and specifically the question of why so many Americans were trying so hard to be happy, led to a natural curiosity of how people in other countries viewed the subject. In the following decades, studies would show that Americans as a group were not the happiest people on the planet, something many could already intuitively sense. Bertrand Russell, the notable British philosopher, was of the mind that Americans, much like citizens of his country, were just not able to take pleasure in their successes in life. Even those fortunate enough to have good health and considerable wealth were often somber in English-speaking countries, he observed for the *New York Times Sunday Magazine* in 1952, describing Americans of this category as displaying "a fundamental malaise." Rather than seeing faces that radiated happiness, which he had expected to find on his trips across the pond, he saw ones that expressed boredom and discontent, cause for him to ponder why.[36]

Americans' dourness crossed social, economic, and gender lines, Russell posited. Businessmen were trapped in jobs they disliked but felt they had to keep because of the money and status they offered, and housewives were intensely jealous of any neighbor who appeared to be on a higher economic or social rung. "Life for almost everybody is a long competitive struggle where very few can win the race, and those who do not win are unhappy," he wrote, with alcohol heavily relied upon in social occasions to convey a sense of happiness. No such gloominess could be found among people who spoke languages other than English, notably the French, Italians, Spanish, and Mexicans, Bertrand maintained, reason for him to propose that there were two main factors for Americans' general inability to exude happiness.[37]

The first one, he suggested, was that anyone who worked in any large organization, whether it be in government, business, or academia, had to be subservient to someone else (even the CEO of a company had a board of directors and shareholders to report to, it could be said, and the president of the United States had a hundred million or so voters to whom to be accountable). The simple fact that one had a boss of some kind confined and constrained Americans' famous spirit for independence and freedom, with any and all original ideas to be inevitably squashed (or stolen) by one's supervisor. There was thus no good reason to try to excel at one's job except by following orders, not a good recipe to make a happy man or woman. Spouses offered little sympathy in this respect, recommending that their husband or wife just play the game to get ahead. "And so you are condemned to gastric ulcers and premature age," Russell quipped, not a far cry from the literally sad truth.[38]

The even bigger reason that most Americans fell on the unhappy side of the fence, according to Russell, was that people in this country tended to "act not on impulse but on some principle." The pressure to conform in postwar America was keeping humans' natural inclination for impulsive action at bay, with the perceived need to follow systematic and uniform principles, causing individuals in this country to, in

Russell's words, "dry up." The corollary was that the most basic principle in the United States at midcentury was to try to get ahead of others, he contended, this too not a good means of realizing happiness because there was always someone else who was "ahead" in some way. "Simple pleasures are destroyed as soon as competitiveness gets the upper hand," he observed, seeing the country's current cultural climate as allowing precious few opportunities for citizens to exhibit the kind of happiness he had expected to find.[39]

Anyone with any familiarity with Thai people recognized that they seemed unusually happy despite having far less money and material things, cause for editors of the *New York Times Sunday Magazine* to investigate the matter further. In 1956, the newspaper asked Sukich Nimmanheminda, a professor at Chuklalongton University in Bangkok, to explain the Thais' formula for happiness, hoping perhaps that American readers could use some of his insights in their own quest to be happier. From Nimmanheminda's piece, it was immediately apparent that Thais' entire philosophy of and approach to life contrasted sharply with that of Americans. Thai people appeared to have little or none of Americans' famous (or infamous) drive for change, progress, and achievement, instead subscribing to an ethos that Nimmanheminda summarized as "leave well enough alone." One's karma, in which one's fate was determined by actions in past lives, was responsible for defeats in Thai life, he explained, a much different story than Americans' penchant to blame themselves (or others) for failure. Religion also played a significant role in the happiness equation. Most Thais were Buddhists, explaining their literally Zen attitude toward life, while most Americans were Christian, a religion in which the prospect of going to Hell after death loomed large if one didn't behave a certain way. Relatedly, Thais did not fear death as Americans did, this alone probably shaping how happiness played out within each culture. Funerals were more social affairs than anything else in Thailand, with little of the demonstrative displays of grief and sorrow often found at those in the United States.[40]

The list of factors that went into Thais' unusual degree of happiness went on and on. Unlike many other countries, Nimmanheminda pointed out, Thailand had never been colonized, giving people there an innate sense of freedom and self-confidence that spilled over into a general feeling of happiness. Visitors to Thailand were often struck by their friendliness, even toward strangers like themselves, and how much of the time they seemed to be smiling. Most tellingly, perhaps, Thais seemed to never be in a hurry, quite different than in the United States, where the term "rat race" was now often being used to describe everyday life. "Had [Americans] known better, or behaved better, they would have been born Thais!" Nimmanheminda remarked, a view that directly challenged our core mythology that we were a chosen people with the highest quality of life of any civilization in history.[41]

The Happiness Rat Race

In part because they came from other countries, Nimmanheminda and Russell were each able to perceive Americans' difficulty with happiness in ways that critics in this country typically could not. The phrase was not yet in parlance, but Americans appeared to be "stressed out," with the pressures of modern life squeezing out much opportunity to find happiness. It was thus not surprising that many Americans were taking tranquilizers (i.e., drugs that relieved tension and anxiety). Sedatives, which slowed down mental functioning, had been around in the United States for decades, but this class of drugs (referred to as "ataraxics" by physicians) made their debut in the country around midcentury. By 1956, some thirty-five million prescriptions for tranquilizers were being written annually, a shockingly high number in such a short period of time. Three out of every ten prescriptions were for what users preferred to call "happiness pills," in fact, the beginnings of the pharmacopeia dedicated to depression and other mental conditions.[42]

Psychiatrists were disturbed by this sudden mass consumption of drugs being taken to swap unhappiness for happiness (one leading pharmaceutical company had advertised its product as a "new and effective means for tranquility, cheerfulness, assurance, optimism, energy, and general well-being").[43] In 1956, the American Psychiatric Association issued a formal statement that warned users of the dangers involved with taking tranquilizers, the most common of them an extract from snakeroot and the other the synthetic chlorpromazine. Relying on medication to relieve "everyday tensions" was not a good idea, the APA advised its ten thousand members, deeming this gobbling up of pills "a public danger." People in show business were especially fond of tranquilizers, finding them useful in making them look relaxed on stage or screen, but businesspeople, lawyers, and who the *New York Times* called "harried housewives" were also avid consumers. The psychiatric community was understandably concerned that the long-term effects of these drugs was unknown until scientific testing could be done, but the possibility that some of its business could be taken away by these quick fixes likely played a role in its action.[44]

Not just psychiatrists but social critics considered "happiness pills" to be a public danger. Writing in *The American Mercury* in 1957, Jess Raley argued that tranquilizing drugs would "nullify man's power to progress" by making us satisfied with the status quo. Without emotions like fear, tension, eagerness, or worry, he suggested, great things would not be achieved, as history clearly showed that necessity often drove people to action. "Had King John been in possession of a good supply of 'happy pills,' he wrote, he might well have distributed them among the nobles and avoided the battle of Runnymede." Progress relied upon the perfectly natural feelings of frustration and discontent, Raley sensibly maintained, emotions that this set of new drugs promised to make disappear like magic. "Since it has become possible for men to annul this frustration artificially and enjoy a simulated happiness without paying the heretofore price," he concluded, "is it not unreasonable to assume that the pace will slacken, cease to move, and begin to slip backward?"[45]

As Bertrand Russell suggested, a big part of Americans' lack of happiness was due to having a job that one disliked if not outright hated. We tend to think of the postwar years as ones in which employees stayed at a single organization for most or all of their careers, but the fact was that Americans were active job-hoppers in this era. Leaving one job for another was "one of the precious rights in a free society under the heading of the pursuit of happiness," wrote Robert G. Whalen for the *New York Times Sunday Magazine* in 1957, observing that "the working men and women of America are exercising it freely these days." In such good economic times, well-paying jobs were in abundance, making the words "I quit" frequently heard in many a corporate hallway, factory, retail store, and just about any other place of business. Earning more money was a strong incentive to go to work somewhere else, of course, but research was showing that job dissatisfaction of one kind or another played a significant, and underappreciated, role in quitting. Just as Russell mused, bad supervision was the most common reason to hate one's job and hope that a new boss would be more empathetic and fair-minded.[46]

Despite all the signs that many Americans were chasing happiness but never quite catching it, our fundamental right to pursue it remained a staple of our national character. Politicians, especially when running for office, frequently could not resist tapping into the rhetorical power of the phrase "the pursuit of happiness," knowing that the words elicited pride in country. Democrats and Republicans typically assigned alternative meanings to the words, however, something that became apparent at all levels of the political arena. The 1956 presidential election, for example, in which Republican incumbent Dwight D. Eisenhower and running mate Richard Nixon campaigned against Adlai Stevenson, former governor of Illinois, and Estes Kefauver, senator of Tennessee, clearly illustrated how the nation's two major parties interpreted the phrase differently. Labeling Jefferson the nation's first Democrat, party leaders adopted the Founding Father's words as the title of a film designed to set up the keynote address at the national convention in Chicago in August. The movie traced the highlights of the party's proud past, beginning with Jefferson penning the phrase in the Declaration of Independence. The writer and narrator of the film was thirty-nine-year-old John F. Kennedy, the senator from Massachusetts, who was getting a lot of attention as a rising star within the party.[47]

Making his way through notable Democrats of the past such as Grover Cleveland, William Jennings Bryan, and Woodrow Wilson (and somehow Abraham Lincoln), Kennedy finally reached Franklin Delano Roosevelt, whose name sparked wild applause from the delegates. FDR had rescued Americans' inalienable right to pursue happiness from what JFK described in the film as "the lowest ebb in our history," just the kind of leadership that was needed now during the Cold War as the country faced an even more dangerous threat.[48] The movie, which was broadcast by NBC and ABC, was well received ("If there must be political films, *The Pursuit of Happiness* established a high standard," noted Jack Gould in his review for the *Times*), but CBS's decision not to include it in its coverage of the convention raised hackles among Democrats.[49]

Political history mattered little to those who believed economic security was the key to personal happiness, however. President Eisenhower saw a direct link between a healthy national economy and Americans' happiness, saying as much as he campaigned for reelection in October 1956. "We see a glow of happiness on people's faces," Ike told an audience in Denver a couple of weeks before the election, taking issue with Democrats' claim that the country was experiencing "false prosperity" and that Americans were a "fearful" people. "America is more prosperous [and] happier than it was four years ago," he continued, celebrating the fact that the nation's economic numbers had indeed risen during his first term. Eisenhower was running on a campaign platform of "Prosperity and Peace," more evidence that he and fellow Republicans perceived a booming economy and strong defense program as the basis for Americans to wake up and go to bed happy.[50]

Carl Sandburg, the Pulitzer Prize–winning poet (and Lincoln historian), could not disagree more. "When the goal of a country is only happiness and comfort, there is danger," the seventy-eight-year-old poet stated in 1956 as the president ran for reelection, riffing on something Albert Einstein had once said regarding his preference for struggle over contentment in life. Rather than being the main instrument of personal happiness, "America's fat-dripping prosperity" posed major peril, Sandburg believed, seeing the nation's keep-up-with-the-Joneses brand of consumerism as a hindrance to versus an enabler of self-fulfillment. As well, satisfaction and complacency were simply not part of the American spirit, he maintained, insisting that it was the desire to continually set and reach for new goals that made people in this country truly happy.[51]

Others perceived the equation of consumption with happiness in the late 1950s as a deviation from our authentic national character. Under the spell of Madison Avenue, Americans were being duped into thinking happiness was a commodity, and using materialism as a cheap substitute for the real thing. "One who thinks of happiness as a thing, can be and wants to be persuaded that there are things for sale to catch it with," wrote George P. Elliott in *The Nation* in 1959, the amount of money one spent and even the thing itself largely beside the point. Happiness was to be found in the buying and owning of something, many Americans were told over and over, whether it was a $1 bottle of Listerine or a luxurious home costing upward of $30,000 at the time. More people had more money than in any place or at any time in history, making it perhaps understandable why so many Americans believed they ought to be happy and were surprised to find that they weren't. "Happiness is an official U.S. product," Elliott claimed, and something that was not just consumed in large quantities domestically but exported through government and corporate propaganda.[52]

With happiness and the American Dream ("a vision of a better, deeper, richer life for every individual, regardless of the position in society which he or she may occupy by the accident of birth," as James Truslow Adams, the coiner of the phrase, defined it in 1933) sharing a kind of symbiotic relationship, it made sense that many Americans felt they had yet to achieve much of either as the 1950s wound down.[53] Social critics were having a field day with Americans' apparent restlessness, with a quick look at the literary bestseller list revealing as much. Vance Packard's *The Status Seekers* was a scathing analysis of our consumerist lifestyle, for example, and Edmund Schiddel's novel *The Devil in Bucks County*, which was heavily based on reality, exposed the darker side of small-town life. Was anyone happy in America? one had to ask, or was the apparent inability for many to achieve their American Dream the cause for such widespread dissatisfaction? "The great American Dream . . . was supposed to lead straight to happiness and contentment," observed John F. Bridge in the *Wall Street Journal* in 1959, thinking that such books suggested that Americans were "so unhappy and discontent that the dream must be a sham."[54]

Happily, so to speak, there was some evidence that at least a few Americans had found happiness by making their American Dream come true. Rather than look to bestsellers that made the nations' inhabitants out to be a status-seeking, insecure bunch, Bridge suggested, readers should look to another, much less popular book just published, *The Delectable Mountains*. In his book, Berton Roueche told the stories of eight people or groups who were doing exactly what they wanted to do in life and, because of that, were by all signs genuinely and thoroughly happy. Long Island potato farmer George C. Strong (who grew the delectable Green Mountain variety of the book's title), Connecticut yoke oxen breeder Percy Beck Beardsley, New York City glass cutter Louis Haft, and the Shakers religious colony were as contented as can be despite the fact that their pursuits of happiness had little or nothing to do with symbols of having "made it." Having no boss and not getting caught up in the competitive, consumerist rat race did indeed appear to be a winning formula for those seeking happiness. This idea would blossom in the next decade, as Americans continued their search for the elusive state of happiness.[55]

WHAT MAKES YOU HAPPY? 1960–1979

We seem to be dedicated to the idea of buying our way to happiness. —John Ciardi, 1964

In October 1979, the *New York Times* informed its many readers of a disturbing finding. A "lag in happiness" had been found in the nation's youth, the newspaper reported, with research showing that young Americans were less satisfied with their lives than their counterparts of a generation ago. "Young people are not as positive as they were 20 years ago," said Angus Campbell of the University of Michigan's Institute for Social Research, the even bigger surprise being that it was the more affluent and better educated who were most likely to be unhappy. Americans younger than thirty years old were less optimistic than those older than sixty, according to the professor of psychology and sociology, a rather shocking piece of information given that it had long been believed that senior citizens represented the least happy segment of the population (because they supposedly had little to look forward to in life). The overall quality of life in the United States had deteriorated since the 1950s, Campbell concluded to explain the study's findings, although it remained unclear what specifically was causing the "lag" in young people's happiness.[1]

Were Americans truly going backward in their search for happiness? It certainly seemed so if young adults, who in theory had much to be happy about, were glum about both their present and future. The 1960s and 1970s would indeed prove to be rocky years for happiness in America, a reflection of that era's major cultural upheaval. Happiness took a sharp turn toward the self in the early sixties as countercultural attitudes and behavior crept into everyday life. It was up to the individual to determine his or her level and kind of happiness, experts were now saying, a shift from the more social or communal version that was in place during the wartime and postwar years. It was even acceptable for an individual to occasionally be unhappy, according to some how-toers, something unlikely to be heard in the put-on-a-happy-face 1950s. The focus on the self would turn out to be not an especially good avenue to lead Americans to greater happiness, however, with this most bewildering of emotions continuing to be a source of frustration for many.

In Pursuit of Happiness

As usual, smart people weighed in on the challenge of being happy in what was an increasingly complex and bureaucratic world. The postwar economic boom was showing few signs of slowing down in 1960, but corporate life was clearly not the best fit for everyone. Many American men were finding themselves in jobs that they didn't particularly like but offered considerable economic rewards and social status, making it a struggle to find happiness in one's work life. For such men, experts advised, it was best to not get caught up in the rat race, and to focus on one's achievements versus doing everything one could to make it the top. "Happiness depends more on progressing and succeeding than on being something or possessing something," wrote F. L. Lucas for *Holiday* that year, thinking the effort spent in pursuing a particular goal was far more fulfilling than getting a key to the executive bathroom. Those who reached their ambitions at an early age often exhausted their possibilities, he added, more reason to not be in such a hurry. "It is usually happier to succeed constantly than spectacularly," Lucas noted, comforting news to the millions of men in gray flannel suits feeling pressure to jockey for promotions and raises.[2]

Research by sociologist Judson T. Landis supported the view that working overtime in order to impress one's boss was not likely to lead to happiness. People were happiest when they were busiest, his studies showed, quite a different thing than striving for externally defined success like a generous bonus or bigger office. Many dreamed of the day they could retire in order to finally "relax," but this also typically proved to be a bumpy road to happiness. As many retirees who had active careers could tell you, playing golf or fishing all day quickly got boring, making them look fondly back on the days when they were frenetically trying to meet a project deadline or beat out the competition to win an account. "Busyness" did appear to be correlated with personal happiness. A study by researchers at the University of Rochester found that businesspeople were the happiest Americans, followed by teachers and clerical workers, all occupations that required a high level of involvement while on the job.[3]

Such studies were part of a more concerted effort within academia and government to learn more about the workings of happiness. "Psychologists, sociologists, and research scientists in leading universities have been exploring happiness from various angles," reported John E. Gibson in *Today's Health*, "and they've come up with some interesting findings." American society as a whole was being closely scrutinized by experts in a variety of fields during the postwar years, in part to gain a better understanding of our way of life in contrast to that offered by alternative political and economic systems, notably socialism and communism. Differences in the kind and degree of happiness between men and women, for example, represented one area of exploration. Which was the happier gender in Kennedy-era America? Psychiatrist David H. Fink suggested that women, who at the time were popularly believed to possess more intense and a wider range of feelings, had the greater capacity for both happiness and unhappiness. Women's highs and lows were each respectively higher and lower than those of men, he argued, his findings no doubt influenced by the common perception that the former were the more emotional sex.[4]

Naturally, the intellectual elite was quite interested in determining whether those deemed smarter than average were happier people. The general assumption was that this was true (i.e., that greater intelligence was linked to greater success and thus greater happiness). Research, however, suggested just the opposite; it was the less intelligent who were happier people. Studies at Ohio Wesleyan University showed that students with higher than average IQs ranked themselves as significantly less happy than those with lower IQs, the explanation being that higher intelligence brought with it a greater awareness of the darker side of life. Findings from a study at the University of California Medical School were much the same. Brainier people had more trouble dealing with the trials and tribulations of everyday life, researchers there reported, and it also took longer for them to bounce back from setbacks.[5]

Other inquiries into happiness in the early 1960s attempted to determine which kinds of Americans were most likely to be happy and why. Physical appearance was understandably an area of interest, the assumption in this case being that better-looking people were happier than average because they could be considered to have a kind of competitive advantage or edge over others. Researchers at Indiana University found that those rated as attractive were indeed among the happiest, although the findings from this study, much like those of many others, would later be challenged based on subsequent research. Of greatest interest to researchers, however, was determining those variables of happiness of which one had some control over, as it was those that offered individuals the opportunity to elevate their subjective state of well-being. Having an optimistic outlook on life, getting regular physical exercise, being grateful for what one had, and avoiding a preoccupation with material things were all steps a person could take to increase his or level of happiness, thinking at the time went, with the ability to live in a sunny place icing on the cake.[6]

The burgeoning arena of happiness research could be said to have reached a critical mass with the publication of "In Pursuit of Happiness" in 1963. Based on what was perhaps the first systematic study of the subject, "In Pursuit of Happiness" broke new ground in terms of gaining the fullest-to-date understanding of what was termed the "ingredients" of happiness. "What makes you happy?" researchers at the National Opinion Research Center at the University of Chicago asked a representative sample of Americans, with the answers to that and many other questions designed to gain new insights into the state of mental health in the country (the full name of the report was "In Pursuit of Happiness—A Pilot Study of Behavior Related to Mental Health"). Why did some people remain cheerful in the face of considerable adversity? Why did others become gloomy at the slightest disappointment or inconvenience? Norman M. Bradburn, the psychologist who led the study, was determined to find out and, in the process, uncover important findings related to emotional well-being in the United States.[7]

Interestingly, Bradburn favored a definition of happiness that veered from the standard one heavily oriented around personal subjectivity. For him, happiness was "the number of positive satisfactions" in one's life, a far more quantitative measure than usually employed. Having enough good things in life added up to a happy individual, Bradburn proposed, with an insufficient number making it likely that a person would not be happy (not being happy was much different than being unhappy, however, he made clear, as "very happy" people were also at times "very unhappy"). Who was happy and who wasn't according to this study? Married men were much happier than those who had yet to get hitched, with even single women happier than the confirmed bachelor popularly believed to be living it up. As well, a couple having a child often did not lead to greater happiness for either spouse, Bradburn reported. Rather than being a "bundle of joy," a newborn frequently created greater con-flict in a household, the findings suggested, challenging another suppo-sition about the constitution of happiness.[8]

Strangely enough, according to "In Pursuit of Happiness," some of those whose lives could be considered a complete train wreck remained happy people, a function of the cumulative nature of happiness. Having a marriage on the rocks, a boss from hell, and a host of other problems did not necessarily produce an unhappy person, in other words, as it was the amount of positive things in life that contributed to happiness. "Maladjustment in social roles is associated only with an increase in negative feelings and not with a decrease in positive feelings," Bradburn explained, good news for those going through a rough patch or worse. Life filled with lemons? Make lemonade by adding lots of sugar, this finding suggested, a heavy dose of sweetness to more than compensate for all the sourness.[9] Individuals should put an "accent on the affirma-tive," as *Changing Times* expressed it in 1963, a reflection of the new responsibility being placed on Americans to take ownership of their personal form of happiness.[10]

Buying Our Way to Happiness

The decidedly touchy-feely brand of happiness that would find full flower in the 1970s could be easily detected in the mid-sixties. June Callwood's 1964 *Love, Hate, Fear, Anger and the Other Lively Emotions* firmly located happiness within the range of key human emotions, while other contemporary authorities on the subject had the audacity to consider happiness a "journey."[11] The standard belief that all Americans had a guaranteed "right" to happiness was even being called into question during these seminal years of cultural change. With more young people in one society than ever before, experts in child raising understandably turned their attention to the role of happiness in human development. A happy childhood was a critical component in the formation of emotionally healthy, well-adjusted adults, studies by psychologists and sociologists showed, helping to seed baby boomers' lifelong, proactive pursuit of happiness.

Some cultural critics, however, notably Joseph Wood Krutch of *Saturday Review*, were highly skeptical about such allegedly scientifically gathered evidence about happiness in America. It wasn't just "In Pursuit of Happiness" that Krutch had a problem with, but rather any attempt to quantitatively calculate the prevalence of a human emotion. "Sociological measurements of contentment . . . are very nearly meaningless," Krutch argued, thinking "In Pursuit of Happiness" might make good literature but had little to do with real science. Researchers like Bradburn occupied "the never-never land of the humanities," Krutch firmly believed, making an effort to measure our national happiness with a "slide rule and calipers" a suspect enterprise at best.[12]

Krutch had a good point. While it was nice to believe that there was a formula to happiness, specifically one in which negative events didn't matter so much as long as there were enough positive events to outweigh them, the truth was probably much more complex. Questionable research practices would prove to be a running theme in the history of happiness, making Krutch's skepticism not so unusual. Bradburn used the phrase "a lot" in his questionnaire and interviews (conducted among two thousand people residing in four small Illinois towns), for example, hardly an objective way to measure anything. Beyond that, Krutch wondered, was happiness the best lens by which to view mental health? Probably not, but most readers, judging by the letters to the editor of *Saturday Review* that followed, were sympathetic to Bradburn's well-intentioned effort to gain more knowledge of what was admittedly a complicated subject. Sociologists in particular were understandably bothered by Krutch's taking pot shots at their field, insisting their methods and analysis were empirically sound.[13]

A much easier way to get a solid understanding of happiness in the United States was simply to examine Americans' active participation in the marketplace. Consumer culture had exploded during the postwar years, as upwardly mobile Americans more than made up for the thrift and sacrifices that were necessary during the Depression and World War II. Since midcentury, the promise of happiness was closely woven into the consumer-oriented American Way of Life, with the market-place of goods commonly seen as the most direct route to pleasure and contentment. Writing for *Saturday Review* in 1964, John Ciardi argued that most Americans looked to the accumulation of possessions as the primary means of becoming happier people. Social status too was heav-ily determined by the version of materialism one was able to afford, making keeping up with the Joneses through consumption a key theme of the postwar era.[14]

As other critics had noted, however, Ciardi believed that the role of the marketplace was more about generating unhappiness than enabling happiness. "The forces of American commercialism are hugely dedi-cated to making us deliberately unhappy," he posited, perceiving the whole purpose of marketers' principle tool—advertising—as "not to satisfy desires but to create them." From an early age, Americans were taught that happiness resided in owning things, the kicker being that material wants were of course limitless. No amount of possessiveness would lead to happiness because there were always many more things to acquire, something Ciardi thought marketers knew all too well based on their perpetual carrot dangling. Completely satisfying consumer wants would be a terrible business strategy, after all, making insatia-bility the key to not just a particular company's continual profitability but the nation's economic growth. The illusion that happiness could be bought was perhaps the biggest weakness of Western society, he pro-posed, joining the ranks of previous cultural critics such as David Ries-man, C. Wright Mills, and John Kenneth Galbraith who had exposed the inherent flaws of consumer capitalism.[15]

Western intellectuals were not the only ones arguing that materi-alism would not lead individuals to the happiness they were seeking. Happiness was a hot topic in China, of all places, in the mid-1960s, with political leaders across the Communist country offering citizens a tutorial in the subject. Commissars, as they were called, were traveling from town to town on a lecture circuit to answer the question "What is happiness?" a response to the encroachment of Western-style consumerism. Genuine happiness could result only from serving the goals of the Communist party, government ambassadors told local attendees, strongly encouraging them to adopt an ideology of austerity. "Collective happiness is above individual happiness, spiritual life is above material life, and the viewpoint of interpreting happiness as personal enjoyment of material comforts of life [should be] discarded," went part of the official message delivered to the proletariat. Interestingly, the aggressive campaign that was labeled "Socialist education" had more to do with economics than anything else. Should the country's seven hundred million people work harder and spend less, leaders in Peking believed, the government could raise the capital that could be used to create a more modern and industrial China. The "Great Leap Forward" program of 1958–1960 had turned out to be just the opposite, pushing officials to try a more ideological approach to the country's economic woes.[16]

In some respects, the Communist party's ambitious effort to provide a (literally) working definition of happiness for hundreds of millions of people was impressive. For millennia, great minds had struggled mightily to put the emotion into language; many deep thoughts about happiness had been produced but no single meaning of the word had ever stuck. Now, however, the Chinese had found one: happiness was labor, and vice versa. The party had actually opened up the matter for debate, with readers of newspapers allowed to voice their thoughts on the subject. All submissions were deemed "wrong," however, with officials then providing the "right" definition in the state-run media. Younger people were expressing interest in material comforts such as books, a radio, fine food, and a wool suit as well as more leisure time, dangerous signs that the generation was drifting toward a bourgeois lifestyle.[17]

China's crackdown on a Western concept of happiness was also in response to an even greater drift taking place in the Soviet Union. China wanted to distance itself from Russia, where citizens were showing clear signs of interest in possessing some of the comforts and conveniences of life, none more than an automobile. The Russians were well on the way to become a major manufacturer of automobiles in an effort to propel its own economic program, and private cars were increasingly popping up on the streets of Moscow. Although the private automobile was the most egregious symbol of the capitalist way of life, a growing number of affluent citizens (including many in the government) were lining up to get one of the Russian-made cars that cost the equivalent of $4,000. Many more longed to own their own car, not just for the convenience one offered but because it functioned as a signifier of high economic and social status. "Happiness is driving your own Moskvich," the *New York Times* reported in 1966, with being seen cruising down Moscow's Gorki Street in the 50-horsepower vehicle inevitably generating many an envious look.[18]

There's Nothing Funny about Happiness

While anyone with a few thousand bucks could walk into a car show-room in the United States and drive out with a vehicle far superior to the Moskvich, government officials were convinced that Americans were not as happy as they could or should be. On August 11, 1965, President Johnson announced his intention to put together a committee to define the nation's goals in health, education, and "happiness" as part of his ambitious "Great Society" social and economic program. Efforts to improve the nation's health and education were certainly understandable, but at least one social critic had to wonder why Washington was getting into the happiness business. "The historic Internal Happiness Act of 1966, which the President signed today in a joyful setting at Disneyland, will throw the full weight of the Federal Government behind man's ancient battle against depression, blues, boredom, Sunday-morning letdown, lackluster marriage and inferiority complex," the columnist Russell Baker quipped. LBJ was on a mission to improve conditions in the country, and was leading legislation to create a more equitable society, notably by reducing poverty and racial injustice. But was elevating Americans' happiness really part of the government's job? Baker was effectively asking, thinking Johnson might be going too far in his noble aims.[19]

Baker could not resist satirizing Johnson's inclusion of happiness within his proposed White House study group and, in a larger sense, the bureaucracy that defined the president's administration. A new cabinet agency, the Federal Happiness Administration, would be formed, Baker continued, with a Secretary of Serenity, Joy, and Contentment to lead that initiative. Other elements of this new program would be a Happiness Corps ("an elite group of college-trained extroverts sent into the field to live and work among the unhappy"), an Office of Happy Operations ("charged with the responsibility of creating happy alternatives for the unhappy"), a Gloom Intelligence Agency (to "ferret out hidden brooders"), and an Internal Happiness Service (to collect a new "glum tax"). "There's nothing funny about happiness," Baker humorously claimed the president stated when the latter was asked about his administration's latest grand plan to level the nation's playing field.[20]

Johnson wasn't the only one to incorporate happiness into the political arena in the 1960s, however. A few years after LBJ's announcement, Vice President Hubert Humphrey, who was vying to become the Democratic nominee for president, defined his campaign platform as a "politics of happiness," suggesting that things were going relatively well in the United States. Humphrey cited statistics such as that Americans owned seventy million television sets to support his position that the country was in general a happy one, an absurd claim by any measure given the state of the nation in 1968. In addition to a growing antiwar movement that was threatening to split the nation in two, poverty, racism, and crime remained prevalent despite the good intentions of LBJ's Great Society domestic programs. Fellow Democratic presidential candidate Robert F. Kennedy was quick to pounce on the vice president's campaign theme. "For those who have affluence it is easy to say this is the politics of happiness," RFK told a crowd in Detroit in May that year, emphasizing that "everything in America is not satisfactory." The New York senator had just won the Nebraska Democratic primary, a good indication that voters agreed that happiness was not a good word to assign to the nation's emotional condition at the time.[21]

As the campaign went on during that spring, Vice President Humphrey defended his "politics of happiness" theme, accusing his opponents of interpreting it as something he did not mean. From his perspective, happiness did not imply frivolity or complacency but rather unity and hope, the latter terms that were entirely consistent with our national character. Senator Kennedy continued to attack Humphrey's campaign theme, however, stating there was no place for widespread happiness in the country while record numbers of Americans were dying in Vietnam. Humphrey, meanwhile, was using the term more carefully in his speeches, even quoting historical figures like John Adams, who had allegedly employed the phrase "the spirit of public happiness" to convey the joy that came with citizenship and self-rule. "You bet, I'm happy," the vice president said in May 1968, declaring that his happiness came from the opportunity to serve his beloved country.[22]

Right on cue, Russell Baker chimed in on the kerfuffle, offering some much-needed lightheartedness to the political squabble. "The Humphrey campaign was scarcely a month old when it became clear that happiness was the most revolutionary innovation in politics since television," he jested, renaming the vice president's theme as "You never had it so happy!" Humphrey and President Johnson had recently appeared on television to sing the Simon and Garfunkel hit tune "Feelin' Groovy," Baker joked, with this public display of happiness having an infectious effect. "People began to feel good again for the first time in years," he continued, "and they discovered that they liked it." Seeing that Humphrey's embrace of happiness was helping him in the primaries, Baker went on, one of his staffers started a rumor that the vice president's opponents, Robert Kennedy and Eugene McCarthy, were each "sourpusses." "I am not now, nor have I ever been, a sourpuss," Kennedy stated, according to Baker, the icing on the cake being that the Republicans, seeing which way the winds were blowing in the Democratic contest, nominated Happy Rockefeller (the wife of Governor Nelson Rockefeller) as their candidate for president.[23]

Not just politicians recognized the semiotic power of happiness in the late 1960s, perhaps because the real thing was in such short supply. Advertising agencies were discovering the linguistic freight of happiness as the sixties wound down, and were increasingly linking the word to brands as a compelling selling point. After taking the TWA account away from Foote, Cone & Belding, for example, the airline's new agency, Wells, Rich, Greene, landed on happiness as its new campaign theme. TWA's last advertising campaign, "Up, Up and Away," had been a memorable one, but now the airline was telling consumers, "Our people make you happy. We make them happy." TWA employees all over the world were beginning to wear buttons reading "When you're happy, I'm happy" to dovetail with the ad campaign and in hopes customers would vote for them in a company-wide contest. Employees who made their customers happiest would receive cash and other prizes, Wells, Rich, Greene announced, thinking the agency was really onto something with this new happiness angle.[24]

Another large Madison Avenue agency, BBDO, was also keen on happiness but was taking a different tack. Rather than pitch happiness to consumers, BBDO decided to try to determine which Americans were happiest, thinking the research would prove useful in developing campaigns for its clients. Knowing consumers inside and out was one of the primary tasks of an agency, after all, and what better way to do that than by learning who were happy and who were not? "What could be more basic than whether our prospects are happier, more satisfied with their life, more content than other segments of the population?" a BBDO spokesman asked in 1972, thinking the best way to answer that question was to interview a few hundred people on the telephone. The results? "If you're looking for a very happy person, look first for a very religious married woman who is between 18 and 34 years of age, making between $8,000 and $14,000 a year with her high school diploma, from a small family and has seven or more friends," the *New York Times* reported after learning the results of the survey. While BBDO was eager to show the business community how it was leading the way in happiness research in the early seventies, the agency did not specify what kind of products this kind of most happy American was likely to buy.[25]

An Unflagging, Unsagging State of Mind

The ascent of happiness in the public arena during the counterculture years went considerably beyond politics and advertising. The ubiquitous smiley face, as well as the commercialization of expressions like "Have a nice day," illustrated the degree to which the concept of happiness could now be found in everyday life in the United States. The self-help movement of the 1970s dovetailed nicely with this individual-focused interpretation of happiness (and psychological profile of much of the "Me Generation"). Mildred Newman's and Bernard Berkowitz's 1971 *How to Be Your Own Best Friend* reinforced the idea that each person was in charge of his or her own happiness, a clear reflection of the era's emphasis on the self whether it was good, bad, or downright ugly.[26] Happiness was also framed within that era's attraction to "naturalness" in all forms, and it was similarly seen as integral to an individual's sense of "balance." Women's magazines, meanwhile, emphasized love and sex as key ingredients of happiness, not too surprising given the tens of millions of twenty- and thirtysomethings who were making those two things a priority in their lives.

The greater interest in happiness as a dedicated field and the growing number of experts offering advice on how to achieve it belied the general lack of understanding of the subject. Most people could tell you when they were happy and when they weren't, but defining or even describing the emotional state was not easy. "Everyone is sure that happiness is desirable," wrote Paul Cameron in *Psychology Today* in 1974, "but no one seems to know exactly what it is." A good number of social scientists believed that being happy in one form or another was our most fundamental drive, making it all the most puzzling why it was so difficult to put the experience into words. Beliefs about the distribution of happiness in the United States remained heavily informed by cultural stereotypes and prejudices. Happiness was popularly considered to be more prevalent among young, male, white, affluent, and nonhandicapped Americans, a reflection of deeply embedded biases regarding age, gender, race, class, and physical and mental ability. But were any of these generalizations true? more researchers were beginning to ask, thinking there was much more work that had to be done given how central happiness was to the human, and especially American, experience.[27]

Over the next few years, a flood of research devoted specifically to happiness, some of it scientifically grounded and some of it considerably less so, poured forth. Surveys, questionnaires, and polls peppered popular magazines in the latter 1970s as researchers tried to determine which Americans were happier than others and why. Happiness was clearly riding on the still booming self-help movement, in which many Americans were expending much time, energy, and money. In no previous time in the nation's history had there been such a focus on the individual and such a profound belief that one could and should claim his or her inalienable right to happiness. "Americans seek happiness with a fierce determination that is matched only by our passion for privacy and independence," wrote the editors of *Psychology Today* in 1975, defining the emotional state as "an unflagging, unsagging state of mind." Driven much in part by baby boomers' competitive ethos and urge to succeed in all aspects of their lives, there appeared to be higher expectations for fulfillment in both one's career and in relationships. Work and play each offered much opportunity for happiness, the media told Americans, the challenge of course being to find it.[28]

Putting their money where their mouth was, the editors of *Psychology Today* decided to collaborate with the psychology department at Columbia University to learn what made Americans happy. By asking its readers "what happiness means to you," specifically "when you feel it, what you think will bring it, why you do—or don't—have it, and how it relates to personality and past," the magazine's staff was confident that the boundaries of the subject would be significantly expanded. A questionnaire consisting of no less than 123 questions developed by two Columbia professors along with nine graduate students was included in the October 1975 issue, with readers asked to anonymously mail their completed surveys to the university's psychology department. A full report of the results would be published in a future issue of the magazine, the editors told its readers, adding that "your candid and thoughtful replies will help us to understand what the pursuit of happiness is all about."[29]

Ten months later, *Psychology Today* delivered on its promise. More than fifty-two thousand readers ranging in age from fifteen to ninety-five had completed and returned the magazine's questionnaire, this itself an indication of the significance of happiness in Americans' everyday life. Happiness was "that elusive mood in your mind, a delicate balance between what you wanted in life and what you got," according to Phillip Shaver and Jonathan Freedman, the two professors who had led the survey. Interestingly, most people who took the time to fill out the six-page questionnaire, stick it in an envelope with a ten-cent stamp, and pop it into a mailbox fell into two very different groups. Happiness was one group's normal condition, with sadness or anguish a rare interruption of their positive state of mind. For others, however, the very opposite was true, with sorrow and struggle the norm. Dividing respondents into two polarized groups was a simple but revealing means of breaking down what was by all accounts a complex subject. There were happy and unhappy people, this research suggested, with all kinds of factors, including one's childhood, relationships, job, and spirituality, contributing to which group one fell into.[30]

Within this overarching framework of the results of the 1975 *Psychology Today* study were more detailed insights into the dynamics of happiness in America (the editors made it clear that the readers of their magazine were younger, more affluent, better educated, and more liberal than the average American, and that respondents were likely to be more interested in the subject than others). Still, there were key findings related to happiness that went far beyond the splitting of the population into two segments. "We discovered that happiness is in the head, not the wallet," Shaver and Freedman wrote, meaning that making more money in order to buy more or more expensive things was not a good way to become happier.[31]

Beyond concluding that happiness was not for sale, the professors discovered a number of other, often surprising findings, such as that unhappy children typically became happy adults, sexual satisfaction was a function of quality versus quantity, and there was no significant difference in the level of happiness between atheists and the religious, homosexuals and heterosexuals, and urbanites and country folk. Most important, working toward a recognizable, achievable goal was an excellent path to take to find happiness, they reported, with the taking of progressive, incremental steps far more fulfilling than aspiring to some externally defined measure of success. "Happiness has less to do with what you have than with what you want," the pair added, recommending that those striving to be happy set their own standards versus pursue those established by others.[32]

While the Columbia team determined that an unhappy childhood did not typically lead to unhappiness in later life, other research suggested otherwise. "A shortage of love in childhood causes people to choose other sources of happiness, such as money, that don't work as well," wrote Jack Horn after reviewing a study done by Robert M. Gordon. Inspired by Erich Fromm, Harry Harlow, and other leading psychologists who had argued that a lack of love in one's youth could cause serious problems down the road, Gordon decided to investigate the matter as his doctoral thesis at Temple University. Gordon documented the degree of love felt in one's past and present among a few hundred students there, and found that it was far and away the most critical determinant of happiness. Students who were raised in an unloving environment assigned far greater value to money as adults than those brought up with much love in their lives, the research showed, with financial resources turning out to be a poor substitute for what they had not received as children. Materialism would not lead them to the happiness they craved, in this respect echoing findings from the Columbia study. Love was "the most important ingredient of happiness," Horn surmised, an observation that resonated not just with the work of some top psychologists but that of hundreds of writers and artists who had expressed much the same idea over the centuries.[33]

Happy People

As the country climbed out of what was one of its lowest points in its history, new efforts were undertaken to figure out what made Americans happy and why. The nation's bicentennial in the summer of 1976 was a particularly opportune time to investigate the enigma of happiness in America. Inspired by the seminal phrase in the Declaration of Independence, editors of the *New York Times* asked their correspondents across the country to find out how representative Americans were engaged in the pursuit of happiness two hundred years after the Founding Fathers made it a permanent feature of our national character. What did the reporters learn? "They found the search [for happiness] is still there, as it was in the very beginning, as vague and amorphous and wispy as ever, no more clearly defined now than then, but still of mesmerizing import in the lives of 215 million Americans who are chasing it—whatever it is—in a multitude of ways," the newspaper informed its readers one day before the bicentennial.[34]

After these inspiring words, the *Times* told the stories of a handful of Americans who were pursuing happiness on their own terms. A woman from Grosse Point Park, Michigan, was the quintessential mother whose version of happiness was inextricably linked with the well-being of her children, for example, while a forty-three-year-old African American jewelry salesman from Jackson, Mississippi, was struggling to recover the happiness he had enjoyed before desegregation in the state's schools nearly ruined his business (most of the man's contracts for school rings were promptly cancelled when white principals replaced black ones after the law was passed). For a four-year-old boy from Americus, Georgia, happiness was being as much as possible like his father, a CBS cameraman who was traveling with nearby resident Jimmy Carter, who was about to announce his candidacy for president. Meanwhile, a twenty-seven-year-old owner of a Greek restaurant in Toledo, Ohio, was working a hundred hours a week but making money, planning his happiness to come in five to ten years when he could hire someone to do his job.[35]

The range of stories that the *Times* reporters uncovered did indeed demonstrate that happiness was, more than anything else, a personal pursuit. Readers also learned of a twenty-nine-year-old woman from Gary, Indiana, who had happily returned to her hometown after finding much professional success in Chicago. "Gary needed me more than Chicago," she simply explained. A farmer in West Fork, Arkansas, meanwhile, was happiest while tinkering with his tractor and various other machinery, while the newspaper's correspondent in Aspen, Colorado, found no shortage of enthusiasts whose happiness derived from skiing, hiking, camping, rafting, jeeping, and myriad other outdoor activities. "Being happy is hard work in Aspen," the reporter pithily informed *Times* readers.[36]

Regardless of the source of happiness, some argued that finding it was a simpler proposition than it seemed to appear. Psychologists and other experts were overthinking the subject, according to more populist sources that made the case that the Sturm und Drang attached to Americans' arduous search for happiness was classic musings of the overly philosophical. Happiness was "easier than you think," the chipper *Saturday Evening Post* told its readers (most of them middle-aged or older), adding that "you owe it to others and others owe it to you." To prove its point, the still popular but decidedly square magazine featured a number of older celebrities who told their personal story of happiness, each of them able to remain upbeat despite the highs and lows of show business. "Even when I'm doing nothing I find a happy reason for not doing it," the eighty-one-year-old George Burns remarked, claiming he was just as happy as when he was struggling during his vaudeville days. If there was one common theme among these famous people, it was optimism. Fifty-year-old Dr. Joyce Brothers felt "every day is better than before," while seventy-four-year-old Lawrence Welk had "too much to look forward to," comments that supported the view that much of happiness resided in looking forward to what tomorrow might be bring.[37]

Such happy talk was certainly inspiring, but researchers remained determined to dig deep into the human psyche to learn the emotional triggers of happiness and unhappiness. For his doctoral thesis at the University of Michigan, Jeffrey Kane found that happiness relied on being fulfilled in all major aspects of life (i.e., in one's job, with family and friends, and while involved in recreational pursuits). Overall fulfillment suffered if things weren't going well in just one of these areas, implying that balance or equilibrium was the key to personal happiness. Unhappiness in one aspect of life carried over to the others, in other words, making it easy to understand why happiness was for many a struggle. A setback at work, an argument with one's spouse, or even one's favorite team going through a particularly bad losing streak could tip the balance of happiness, this study suggested, our minds apparently programmed to focus on problems as perhaps a kind of survival mechanism.[38]

Other theories about happiness among Americans emerged with the publication of Jonathan Freedman's *Happy People*. Freedman, the Columbia University professor who had co-led the *Psychology Today* research project a few years back, remained interested in who was and wasn't happy and why, and pushed his findings from the landmark study further in the 1978 book. Freedman had what was unarguably a gold mine of research into the subject at his disposal, as the responses from the *Psychology Today* questionnaire were combined with those from a similar survey published in *Good Housekeeping* to generate a total of almost one hundred thousand responses. Readers hoping there would be a simple formula or recipe to happiness presented in the book would be disappointed, however, as artificially producing the emotion just didn't work, Freedman explained. One could have all the typical social and economic ingredients for happiness but still be miserable, he made clear up front, or, completely conversely, be thoroughly happy without having any of them. Happiness was a function of how an individual responded to environmental conditions rather than the conditions themselves, his extensive investigation showed, making one's approach to life the key to how happy one was likely to be.[39]

In his book, Freedman presented a number of leading theories about happiness, and then measured their validity against his research findings. He was quick to discount the popular "comparison" theory of happiness, in which individuals determined how happy they were or weren't in relation to other people. Rather than being absolute, in other words, happiness was relative, this theory went, not unlike how economic or social status was often believed to work. Because we lived in groups, humans measured whatever they possessed in relation to that of others, many an anthropologist argued, making it easy to transfer the theory to the arena of happiness. But that was just one piece of the story, Freedman thought, as his research showed that a good number of people had no interest in comparing common elements to happiness— sexual satisfaction, say—to what others possessed. "The absolute scale seems to me to work for internal states that contribute to happiness," he stated, thinking that "comparisons to others are largely irrelevant."[40]

Freedman also did not heavily subscribe to the "expectation" theory of happiness, in which individuals measured how happy they were based on the "spread" between what they hoped for and what they had actually realized. Individuals with a narrow spread possessed a high level of happiness, according to this theory, as they were getting most or all that they wanted in life. Conversely, those with big gaps between their expectations and reality were unhappy people, as life was just not turning out to be as good as they had believed. While there was some validity to this idea, Freedman explained, the expectations-versus-achievements theory was, like the comparison theory, not the basis for most people's happiness. In his research, Freedman found individuals who had reached or surpassed all their goals in life but remained despondent, supporting his view that the population was generally sorted into happy and unhappy people. "They continue to view life as an unhappy state," he wrote of these unfortunate folks, more reason to subscribe to his contention that "attitudes toward life determine how much we enjoy what happens to us and what we achieve."[41]

While not totally dismissing the comparison- or expectation-based theories of happiness, Freedman leaned more to one in which adaptation played a significant role. Like all organisms, humans adapted or got used to their environment, with this normal process providing a kind of benchmark level of happiness for each individual. We became happier people when the circumstances of life exceeded our adaptation level, according to this theory, and unhappier people when things fell below that level. An increase in happiness could thus be realized only by surpassing our adaptive state in some way, suggesting that we had to continually shake things up at least a bit in our lives if we hoped to become ever happier. "This theory explains why people who seem to have everything are not necessarily happy," Freedman wrote, an idea that supported the fact that money was not strongly linked to happiness. The apparent luxury of having all of one's needs and desires met was therefore not a particularly good enabler of happiness, something that might have come as a surprise to those wishing they could be in someone else's (more pricey) shoes.[42]

Related to the adaptive theory of happiness was the concept that each individual was fundamentally a work in progress, making the common pursuit of becoming a happier person a mostly lost cause. As Maslow had proposed in his hierarchy of needs, humans strive to achieve a higher state of being once a certain level of needs are met, turning life into an endless climbing of an existential ladder. While a good thing in terms of personal evolution, this continual reaching for something "higher" was not at all an effective agent of happiness in that one was never satisfied or fulfilled in the present moment. Freedman believed that this theory helped explain why so many people remained frustrated in their efforts to achieve happiness regardless of how hard they tried. "Once attained for a moment, it seems to slip from one's grasp and be just around the bend," he observed, an apt description of the elusive nature of happiness.[43]

Finally, Freedman believed, based on his interpretation of some hundred thousand accounts of personal happiness, that some people were simply better at being happy than others. There was thus a sort of talent attached to being happy, just as achieving anything in life required having a certain aptitude or set of skills to actually get it done. Why some people had this ability and why others didn't remained a total mystery, but there did seem to be some validity to the idea that happiness was either a competence developed over time or a gift that one was lucky enough to be born with. Freedman had perhaps more insights into the subject than anyone else on the planet, but he readily admitted that he had yet to crack the code of happiness. "Happiness is an enormously complex concept and feeling," he concluded in his *Happy People*, thinking there was still much work to be done in the field to try to solve one of life's greatest puzzles.[44]

The Most Subtle and Elusive of All Human Moods

Freedman's keen insight into the nooks and crannies of happiness, which was supported by what had to be the most complete research study ever employed in the area, did not go unnoticed. Not just fellow psychologists but the mainstream media recognized *Happy People* as representative of the new kind of work being done in the expanding field of happiness. Because the book was grounded in research methods that were far superior to those used in the past and authored by an Ivy League academic, Freedman's work was considered to be, in a word, scientific. Happiness had long been located within the domain of philosophy or literature or religion, making a scientific study of the subject somewhat revolutionary. "Science has begun to nose around in that shifty terrain it so long neglected," observed Frank Trippett in *Time* in 1979, describing happiness as "that most subtle and elusive of all human moods." The presence of hundreds of self-helpers over the years had also not helped in terms of lending legitimacy to the field, this too making work like Freedman's stand out. "The feel-good trade's blizzard of lighter-than-air tracts proves nothing whatever about happiness except that a lot of people are willing to pay for help in pursuing it," Trippett remarked.[45]

Indeed, by the end of the seventies, so much happiness advice had been given out that it was ripe for satire. Riffing on Wayne Dyer's 1976 #1 bestseller, *Your Erroneous Zones*, which purported to show readers how to escape the trap of negative thinking and take control of their lives, Johannes Eff produced a piece a few years later titled "Your Erroneous Bones" for the *National Review*. Eff's "erroneous bones" were much like Dyer's "erroneous zones," which the latter defined as "whole facets of your approach to life that act as barriers to your success and happiness." "Being unhappy makes you sad" and "thinking is very thought-provoking" went a couple of Eff's pearls of wisdom, the irony being that such observations were not all that different from the actual ones being generously doled out at the time. Eff wrote perfectly serious self-help books like *Self-Rescue* under the name John Kantwell Kiley, indicating that he was fully aware that truth was not much different from fiction when it came to to this literary genre.[46]

While happiness advice had represented a sizable segment of the enormous self-help business for at least the last half-century, it had been only relatively recently that the subject had become "in" within the social science community. A few psychological and sociological forays into the science of happiness had been made in the 1960s under the umbrella of mental health, but the social and economic turmoil of the latter half of that decade and the first half of the next had all but squashed serious investigation of the subject. Americans were simply not particularly interested in hearing about happiness during the counterculture era despite the popular calls to "do one's own thing" and "love the one you're with." "Happiness itself was all but out of style in the days of Vietnam, urban riots and the burgeoning dope culture," Trippett explained, the assassinations of Robert F. Kennedy and Martin Luther King, Watergate, the energy crisis, and "stagflation" other good reasons Americans were not wearing smiley faces these years.[47]

Now, however, with those major bummers becoming a bad memory and the nation pulling out of its cultural malaise, happiness was fast becoming one of the hot fields in which to be involved. "Gladness is likely to be subjected to the same methodical research and analysis that has been lavished for generations on our madness," Trippett continued, with academics and practitioners from a variety of disciplines choosing happiness as the focus of their work. Lionel Tiger, an anthropologist at Rutgers, had a new book coming out titled *Optimism: The Biology of Hope*, for example, and Willard Gaylin, a New York City–based psychoanalyst, had recently completed a study called *Feelings: Our Vital Signs*. Each of these works was somehow centered around happiness, the former its possible biology and the latter its emotional basis. As well, researchers at the University of Michigan's Institute for Social Research were continuing their examination of how income and education related to happiness, still believing that there were demographic variables at work in what made certain Americans happy and others not so.[48]

Nearly everybody appeared to be getting into the happiness game at the end of a decade in which individualism had ruled. Change, however, was in the air. *Playboy* had just published the results of a Louis Harris poll probing the sources of happiness, perhaps surprising the magazine's readers by reporting that American men ranked family life as significantly more fulfilling than sexual satisfaction.[49] In her 1979 extensive study of happiness among young men for *Esquire*, Gail Sheehy found much the same, evidence that the seemingly odd finding reported in *Playboy* was no fluke. Readers of *Esquire* told Sheehy (via a questionnaire and/or interview) that the highest degree of happiness came not from work, sex, or money but from having children. Young fathers especially felt that way, with the vast majority of those who had yet to have children wanting to do so. The unhappiest young men, meanwhile, were those who planned to stay single and childless, a finding that suggested self-absorption was not conducive to being a happy individual. A backlash against the hedonistic ways of the last decade seemed to be in play, as baby boomers entered their thirties en masse and yearned to settle down into traditional domestic life.[50]

While all agreed that the wider interest in happiness being expressed by researchers with solid credentials was a positive thing, it was obvious that the field was still in its infancy. Freedman had offered intriguing and well-informed theories about the workings of happiness, notably, but practical information for how to actually achieve it based on hard research was in short supply. "The overwhelming finding of all the research is that there is no easy solution, no foolproof strategy for finding it," Freedman himself admitted, with even a precise definition of happiness still yet to be produced (researchers made no attempt whatsoever to glean a definition from subjects themselves). Efforts to slice up the pie of happiness by geography, financial status, age, marital status, or even health were an equivocal bust, as the most scientifically robust studies indicated that there were no discernible differences along any of these demographically defined measures.[51]

A look back at the last two decades revealed that, while much good work had been done to gain a deeper understanding of happiness in America, the field remained a scattered and nebulous one. Happiness was a "young science," it could safely be said, its current stage equivalent perhaps to that of biology in the fifteenth century or chemistry in the seventeenth. As well, supposedly breakthrough findings in the field, such as having an unhappy childhood, didn't mean one that one was destined to never be happy, or that happiness could be attained with money, could be seen as dolled-up rehashings of centuries-old folklore. The barrage of self-help advice geared toward happiness was also doing the field no favors. Meaningless, silly observations like "It is . . . good to 'feel good,'" an actual sentence in Gaylin's study, made it clear that the science of happiness had a long way to go. "Happiness, in short, awaits its Newton, its Galileo," Trippett concluded, wondering if the subject, much like love and wisdom, was simply beyond a deep level of human comprehension.[52] With the 1980s just around the corner, however, there were signs of a new and different kind of happiness emerging in America, one in which external factors would play a much bigger role.

DON'T WORRY, BE HAPPY, 1980–1999

The elusive Holy Grail of happiness has become the great American obsession. —Taki Theodoracopulos, 1983

In July 1988, the improvisational jazz singer Bobby McFerrin released a single called "Don't Worry, Be Happy." The song (whose title was borrowed from Meher Baba, an Indian spiritual leader, who frequently used the phrase when communicating with his followers) became #1 on the Billboard Hot 100 in September. "Don't Worry, Be Happy" sold ten million copies that year and won the Grammy Award for Song of the Year. Noting that millions of Americans of all ages appeared to be singing or humming what *Newsweek* called a "musical prescription for inner peace," Republican presidential candidate George Bush (unsuccessfully) tried to adopt the song as his campaign theme. A book titled *Don't Worry, Be Happy* with a first print run of one hundred thousand copies was quickly published, with McFerrin adding twenty new verses. A few months later, Bloomingdale's opened a "Don't Worry, Be Happy" shop in its flagship store in New York, where customers could purchase smiley face T-shirts, smiley face jeans, and smiley face boxer shorts.[1]

What was behind the mega-popularity of "Don't Worry, Be Happy" other than its being the first a cappella song to reach the #1 spot on the top 100? The United States was positively happiness happy in the late 1980s, one could easily say, its pursuit never greater in the nation's two-hundred-plus-year history. Millions of Americans were actively searching for true happiness, no doubt finding the song's title and lyrics to be a font of wisdom they could hopefully apply in their everyday lives. McFerrin soon tired of the song, vowing to never perform it again if he didn't have to, but many ordinary Americans clung to it for years, wondering how they could put their worries aside and realize their happiest selves.[2]

Oblique, Ephemeral, and Elusive

Worries were definitely on most Americans' minds a decade earlier. It might have been "a new morning in America," as one of presidential candidate Ronald Reagan's more memorable 1980 campaign commercials stated, but a lingering recession was not helping Americans' concerted efforts to find their personal happiness. Economic woes, like double-digit inflation and a high rate of unemployment, as well as rising crime and the growing threat of the Soviet Union, were good reasons for Americans to wear frowns rather than smiles on their faces as the Reagans moved into the White House in January 1981. But the fact was that average happiness levels in the United States had hardly moved since the heady days of the late 1950s, when anyone, assuming he was male and white, had a good chance of realizing his own American Dream. With a quarter century of data now available, it was becoming clear that economic swings and political events had little or no effect on individual happiness, a curious thing for those trained to believe that people's emotional states were heavily shaped by social forces. "What we are measuring in surveys of happiness and psychological well-being is intimate, personal, private," noted Andrew M. Greeley of the National Opinion Research Center, surprised as anyone how each American defined happiness in his or her own terms.[3]

With happiness viewed through such an individualistic lens, it was not surprising that pleasure was recognized as a defining characteristic of one's relative state of well-being. The early 1980s picked up where the self-oriented, hedonistic 1970s left off, making pleasure in an infinite array of forms the centerpiece of many Americans' pursuit of happiness. The anti-establishment streak of the counterculture was giving way to a new, more conservative set of values, however, one in which pleasure had much to do with how much money and power one had. "Pleasure, then, is for many of us happiness," wrote Robert Coles, a research psychiatrist at Harvard in 1983, "pleasure in possessions, and pleasure in the capital we've accumulated, and pleasure in the authority we wield over others." In his research, Coles found the words "having" and "owning" were frequently mentioned by subjects when discussing happiness, with even children often perceiving their desired future in terms of what they hoped to "get" in life.[4]

While pleasure was, for the moment at least, equated with happiness, anyone hoping to have a genuinely firm grasp of the subject was inevitably frustrated by its slipperiness. "Like most people, I am not sure what happiness is," admitted Taki Theodoracopulos in *Esquire* in 1983, thinking that any attempt to define the term was a futile pursuit. Part of the reason why it was so difficult to understand happiness was because it was a relatively new area of study, he believed. Simple survival was the focus on mankind prior to the twentieth century, Theodoracopulos argued, making the parsing of happiness a luxury that most people for most of human history could not afford. As well, happiness was "oblique, ephemeral, and elusive," he continued, its ability to come and go without warning making an intimate familiarity with the subject that much more challenging.[5]

For Theodoracopulos, happiness had become a much more complex proposition over the past generation. During the postwar years, he posited, happiness was part and parcel of the American Dream, and could be measured by whether one had achieved upward mobility and the material rewards of the so-called good things in life. That narrative of happiness was interrupted by the counterculture, however, making it more difficult to know if one was or wasn't happy. The result was a flourishing industry dedicated to helping Americans find happiness or, at least, help them know where they might find it. "It is the trendiest of anxieties," he wrote of this uncertainty surrounding happiness, "and to prevent it, a whole industry of shrinks, gurus, and books has sprung up and is doing a brisk business." Unfortunately, all this advice appeared to be doing little to make Americans any happier. "We have finally reached a state of such anxious discomfort over how to be happy that our lives have dwindled into an unending process of fulfilling obsessive lists," Theodoracopulos observed, thinking one's degree of self-improvement had become the new measure of happiness.[6]

Paul L. Wachtel, a psychologist at the City University of New York, agreed that happiness was most apparent in the United States during the postwar years (1957, to be exact) because it was so connected to external measures of success. Now, however, in the early 1980s, materialism was not the means by which most people would find happiness, something that would likely come as a surprise to the growing number of Americans on the "fast track" who were determined to keep up with the Joneses and then some. More was less in our age of hyperconsumption, Wachtel argued, our appetites too large to ever feel satisfied. Rather, as he argued in his *The Poverty of Affluence*, personal happiness resided in having a sense of community and adopting a "psycho-ecological" philosophy, presciently anticipating the full-scale environmental responsibility movement that lay ahead. In another sense, the book was a throwback of sorts to the minimalist kind of thinking that was popular in the late 1960s and 1970s, when a good number of young people (rhetorically at least) rejected the consumer-based way of life of their parents' generation.[7]

The writer Anthony Brandt was equally convinced that the upwardly mobile American Way of Life was not a particularly reliable path leading to happiness. "We Americans identify the pursuit of happiness with the pursuit of success, money, and achievement," he wrote in *Esquire* in 1984, with most people assuming they would be happy when they "made it." Brandt did not recognize a direct or even indirect relationship between aspiration and happiness, however, using his father as a prime example. Brandt Sr. had held the same job at the same company for decades and had no further ambitions, he explained, the man "perfectly content" to remain an assistant manager for his entire career. Brandt Jr., on the other hand, found happiness only in his struggle to succeed, making him question our national ethos of striving to accomplish greater and greater things. "The pursuit of happiness feels to me sometimes like a dog chasing its tail," he concluded, wondering if Americans' celebrated effort to get ahead was simple greed.[8]

Running parallel with Americans' eager pursuit of happiness in the 1980s was a significant and growing amount of social pressure to be recognized as a happy person (so many Americans said in surveys and questionnaires that they felt such pressure that *Mademoiselle* reported a new condition it labeled "happiness anxiety").[9] Being labeled as an unhappy individual, whether or not one actually was such a person, was a social stigma that many understandably wanted to avoid. Unhappiness suggested failure, in that the individual had somehow fallen short in seizing his or her inalienable right to pursue happiness as promised in the Declaration of Independence. "To be happy in America is to be literally all right," thought Lesley Hazleton, author of *The Right to Feel Bad*, "and to be unhappy, all wrong." It was certainly odd and disturbing that others judged one's emotions, and that unhappy people were often viewed in negative terms. What was it about that particular personal trait that made people react so strongly? one could ask, the answer of course residing in the degree of importance Americans assigned to happiness.[10]

The estimated 5 to 15 percent of Americans who suffered from depression were most vulnerable to this moral decree against unhappiness. Depressed people were not just in violation of one of our most precious liberties, but were to be avoided, perhaps out of the fear that the condition could be contagious and turn happy people into unhappy ones. "Where we have made happiness into a white knight in shining armor," Hazleton observed in 1984, "we have made depression into a filthy ogre whose shadow hovers threateningly over our lives." Feeling good was praised while feeling bad was vilified, making depressed people ashamed of what was typically a chemical imbalance. Not surprisingly, then, attempts to rid oneself of depression, which could be considered severe unhappiness, was becoming big business as Big Pharma recognized its huge potential. A new generation of antidepressant drugs, including Elavil and Tofranil, were replacing Valium, the beginnings of what would be called Prozac Nation a decade later.[11]

How Americans Pursue It

That happiness was a subjective, personally defined experience was made clear by the number and range of paths Americans were now taking to realize it. The individualistic nature of happiness was made even more so by the fact that people were often finding different ways to be happy at different stages of their life. The life of a typical American in the late twentieth century could even be described as a constantly shifting search for optimal happiness, with each individual continually altering his or her course to try to be a little (or a lot) happier. Cultural and social factors played an important role in providing an overarching framework for an individual's unique route to happiness, especially in early adulthood when one's identity became fully formed.[12] The time and place in which one was living thus set the parameters for happiness by either enabling or constraining an individual's pursuit to be happy. The possibilities to find happiness were arguably never greater than in the United States in the 1980s, as Americans again celebrated their freedoms and liberties and as the economic winds began to shift in their favor.

The opportunity to pursue happiness may never have been greater than in 1980s America, but the pressure to realize it was also likely never greater. Upward of 90 percent of Americans claimed to be happy when surveyed, but their behavior clearly suggested otherwise. Americans were looking anywhere and everywhere to find happiness, with a bewildering array of potential paths to take. Choosing a wrong path could result in an individual being judged by others as an unhappy person, a major social stigma these days when happiness carried so much social currency. The search for happiness was now a huge industry, another sign that Americans were being less than accurate in describing themselves as happy people.[13]

In such a cultural climate, one could see how self-help gurus such as Gail Sheehy and Wayne Dyer found large and receptive audiences eager to hear how they could navigate their way to happiness. Americans had become "gluttons for happiness," according to Joan Juliet Buck in *Vogue* in 1984, our appetite for pleasure and ways to try to achieve it never greater. The devout firmly believed that being virtuous would lead to happiness, while hedonists found that being "bad" made them happiest. "There are those who think that happiness is a reward that must be earned," Buck observed, "and those who think that happiness is a treat that must be grabbed."[14] Others went even further by arguing that Americans were "addicted" to happiness, with no amount of pleasure able to satisfy their desire.[15] Finding happiness in romantic relationships and with one's family remained major challenges, research showed, suggesting that Americans might indeed be fighting a losing battle when it came to trying to become contented people. Harold Kushner's *When All You've Ever Wanted Isn't Enough* astutely addressed the problem that many Americans were confronting with regard to happiness. "Having it all" for some was simply not enough, Kushner had found, with no clear solution in sight.[16]

Thinking there was a large gap between what Americans were saying and actually doing when it came to happiness, the editors at *U.S. News & World Report* wisely decided to further investigate the matter. In a March 1985 special report titled "Happiness: How Americans Pursue It," nine Americans told their own story of happiness, illustrating that reaching that state of emotional well-being was very much a personal affair. For a forty-seven-year-old woman from Cambridge, Massachusetts, for example, obsessive self-improvement was the avenue to happiness, while a career-driven couple from Newport, Rhode Island, found their happiness after moving to a small town in Montana.[17] A twenty-five-year-old man in suburban Pittsburgh, meanwhile, had discovered his version of happiness running a fundamentalist Christian radio station, while a forty-seven-year-old oil executive from Houston was happy as a clam to be a self-proclaimed workaholic.[18] Happiness could be found in status, success, family, religion, knowledge, health, nature, serving others, or any number of other ways, these stories demonstrated, suggesting it was directly linked to one's passion(s) in life.[19] Loving what you do and doing what you love was the key to happiness, one could reasonably conclude, the trick of course being the ability to realize the life of one's dreams.

While some Americans had discovered how to be happy, the United States still lagged behind other countries in terms of overall happiness. Studies of relative happiness among people of different nationalities continued to be undertaken by sociologists in different parts of the world, adding to this line of inquiry that had begun in the 1960s. It was then that social scientists in Europe first conducted the World Values Surveys, in which citizens in various countries were questioned about how happy they were or were not.[20] The latest study published in 1985 put the Republic of Ireland at the top of the list, with their neighbors in Northern Ireland finishing a close second, rather surprisingly. Britain, the Netherlands, and Denmark followed, with the United States coming in at a respectable #6 on the list. Spain, West Germany, Japan, and Italy finished last, this too somewhat surprising given the romantic, fun-loving image of both the Spanish and Italians. Naturally, theories on why the Irish were measurably happier than Americans were promptly proposed, particularly because the former had about one-third per capita income of the latter.

Was it the strong religious faith of the Irish that led to their high level of happiness? some wondered, or, conversely, their penchant of having a pint or two at the local pub after work?[21]

The fact that the United States was not a superpower in happiness was all the more reason for some of America's best and brightest to try to figure out why. The study of happiness had blossomed over the course of the last decade and a half, as psychologists recognized the magnitude of the subject in everyday life (it wasn't until 1973 that the editors of *Psychological Abstracts International*, the leading guide to literature in the field, indexed happiness). Advances in genetics were also leading to some interesting theories regarding the science of happiness. Unhappiness had a strong genetic component while happiness did not, according to a new study led by Edward Diener of the University of Illinois, the former mostly a function of nature and the other mostly of nurture. The research suggested that happiness and unhappiness were thus not, as logic dictated, opposite or inverse emotions; rather, the two appeared to operate independently, and had no clear relationship with each other. Ridding oneself of some unhappiness in one's life therefore did not mean that one would become any happier, somewhat oddly, a counterintuitive notion that threw a monkey wrench into much of the out-with-the-bad, in-with-the-good brand of self-help being cast about. The good news was that, at least according to this research, happiness was not genetically preordained, and could thus be achieved by those who were determined or lucky enough to find it.[22]

Indeed, an army of academics could not slow down the barrage of happiness advice raining down on Americans. Anecdotal evidence suggested that when asked what was the most important thing in life, about half of Americans replied happiness, explaining why the industry dedicated to it was so big. A more specific reason why the market for happiness in this country was so large was because many Americans often mistook the means to achieving it as the ends. For example, success, however defined, was a primary objective for most Americans, it's fair to say, the presumption being that becoming a successful person would lead to happiness. That wasn't always or even likely often the case, however; the quest for success could be so consuming in itself that there was no opportunity to address the real goal of happiness. "People spend so much time making the journey to happiness that they fail to realize it is the journey itself that is happiness," observed Ardath Rodale, CEO of

Rodale Press and author of *Climbing Toward the Light*, suggesting that high achievers allow themselves "the freedom of living in the present moment."[23] Focusing on the journey versus the destination wasn't an easy thing, however, making it area on which self-help gurus focused when advising happiness seekers.[24]

Academics like Diener were not above dabbling in happiness advice, albeit in a more scholarly way. Diener along with two colleagues at Illinois, Edward Sandvik and William Pavot, had just written an article about happiness for a book called *Subjective Well-Being*, which offered readers commonsense tips based on their research. People who were in loving relationships, kept busy, were physically active, helped others, and remained open to change scored highest on happiness, they explained, suggesting that the less happy should try to incorporate those things in their lives. Most important and most interesting, the team pointed out, don't try to be too happy; doing so would be likely to lead to both highs and lows, meaning slow and steady was the best pace by which to win the happiness race.[25]

The Mysteries of Feeling Good

The many questions surrounding happiness were made even more perplexing in that wealth appeared to be almost irrelevant. With all the changes that had taken place in American culture from the postwar years to the early 1990s, most notably the greatest economic boom in history, the happiness needle hadn't budged. One-third of Americans said they were "very happy" in 1957, the very same percentage as in 1993, according to the National Opinion Research Center of the University of Chicago. The country's GNP had nearly doubled over that stretch of time as had per capita consumption, yet such economic measures apparently had little to do with happiness. As well, a case could be made that not only did greater personal wealth not lead to greater happiness, but its pursuit got in the way of actually realizing it. Working longer hours typically comes at the cost of spending time with family and friends, after all, and it is the latter that is more likely to lead to happiness versus having more money.[26]

Despite all the evidence suggesting otherwise, most Americans remained convinced that having more money would make them significantly happier people. In surveys, a 25 percent raise was often mentioned as the magic number that would make them much happier, but the truth was that the emotional high from such a fortuitous development would last only briefly. One's new income level quickly became the standard for happiness, making another large raise seen as the necessary means to get truly happy. Why did Americans persist in believing money was the most direct route to happiness when it simply wasn't true? "The market culture teaches us that money is the source of well-being," observed Robert E. Lane in *The Public Interest* in 1993, one's relative degree of wealth the most objective and conspicuous way to measure happiness. As well, Americans were not known for their ability to openly talk about the more complex things that made them happy or unhappy, such as their relationships with spouses and children or their victories and defeats at work.[27]

With money off the table, so to speak, researchers continued to search for the essential ingredients of happiness, hoping perhaps that it could be distilled down into a recipe that anyone could use. Psychologists considered happiness to be a subjective state of well-being, meaning there was no single formula to it, but that wasn't stopping scientists from trying to add some objectivity into the mix. Close relationships, a happy marriage, and religious faith were now most correlated with happiness in the United States, with Americans saying they fell on the left-hand side of a happy–unhappy scale three-fourths of the time.[28] With most Americans claiming to be happy most of the time, the question of whether happiness was hardwired into our genetic code as a kind of survival mechanism was raised. Were human beings biologically "programmed" to approach life in a positive manner, some researchers were beginning to wonder, our perpetual pursuit of happiness a clever evolutionary device designed to keep us moving forward, especially when the going got rough?[29]

Such questions revealed the increasing value of the study of happiness to those working in the social sciences, especially psychologists. Over the course of its first century, the field of psychology was centered around "negative" emotions like anxiety and depression, but now those in the field had turned much of their attention to the "positive" side of the human mind. Recognizing that achieving happiness, rather than just avoiding sadness, was of great importance to most people, especially Americans, a younger generation of researchers was determined to dig deeper into the subject. What made one person happy and another unhappy? How did race, gender, class, and age relate to happiness? Work, friendships, and religion likely had something to do with one's level of happiness, but exactly how?[30]

The new focus on the brighter side of human personality represented nothing less than a turning point in psychology. "An international avant-garde is studying happiness," Ariane Barth reported in *World Press Review* in 1993, "drawing the scorn of their problem-oriented colleagues." "Happyologists," as they were sometimes referred to, were especially interested in the connection between happiness and psychobiology (i.e., the chemical goings-on in the body). For millennia it was believed that happy people were more likely to be healthy and vice versa, but now it was becoming clear that there was a biochemical basis for such folklore. Endorphins, particularly serotonin, had a direct effect on the body's immune system, explaining the perceived link between happiness and health. The greater understanding that biology played a large role in governing how happy one was or wasn't helped explain why extreme events in people's lives, whether positive or negative, had just a temporary effect on an individual's relative happiness. The euphoria resulting from an especially positive event and the despair resulting from a particularly bad one each would soon fade, in other words, as the body's natural chemistry took over in determining one's normal happiness level.[31]

The ascendance of psychobiology as a determinant of relative happiness did little to stop the flood of theories proposed to, as Barth expressed it, "unlock the mysteries of feeling good."[32] One more formulaic prescription of or to happiness seemed to come out of an accounting textbook. Having more positive experiences than negative experiences in life put one in the black on a balance sheet of happiness, this one went, making it the mission of any individual to accumulate more assets than liabilities if he or she desired to be happy. A twist on this theory assigned weights to each positive or negative experience, with lots of the former (e.g., good job, happy marriage, enjoyable hobbies) able to outweigh a few of the latter (e.g., personal or professional setbacks). A financial metaphor to happiness could go further. Much like putting away a little money on a regular basis to ensure financial security, small contributions of happiness added up to a tidy nest egg; this approach was considered far wiser than striving to achieve a huge amount of happiness in one fell swoop (á la winning the lottery or embarking on a whirlwind romance).[33]

Other experts in the subject focused more on a particular behavioral trait that they believed represented the key to happiness. John Reich of Arizona State, for example, held that feeling that one was in charge of one's life was the crucial criterion of being happy. "I believe that happiness is being aware not only of the positive events that occur in your life but also that you yourself are the *cause* of these events," he wrote in 1994, "that you can create them, that you control their occurrence, and that you play a major role in the good things that happen to you." The sense that one was operating the rollercoaster of life, rather than just being just a passenger along for the ride, in other words, was for him the basis to well-being. Alex C. Michalos of the University of Guelph in Ontario, Canada, on the other hand, saw happiness as "a relatively long-lasting, positive feeling and attitude." His research showed that the best road to happiness resided in having "a portfolio of desires and interests," meaning a balanced mix of short-term and long-term pursuits in life. Enjoying a regular set of small pleasures and having a few major goals to chase was for Michalos an ideal brew of happiness, a relatively easy and appealing way to view the thorny concept.[34]

Overlooked in such well-intentioned, evidence-based musings on the whats and hows of happiness was the possibility that Americans were simply going about it the wrong way. Our "right to life, liberty and the pursuit of happiness" as stated by Jefferson was undeniably beautiful rhetoric, everyone would agree, but perhaps words that were taking Americans down a road that would ultimately lead to disappointment. It was specifically the "pursuit" of happiness where the problem lay, some argued, as chasing that desirable state of being was not a good means of actually achieving it. Rather, happiness "happened" to certain individuals, this idea went, with no amount or kind of pursuit able to make it happen. Americans' well-known can-do spirit and their deserved reputation to purposely act and accomplish things, whatever the cause, may thus be a fine ethos by which to create successful citizens and a prosperous nation, but it was a poor system when it came to being happy. Happiness was an elusive thing, making Americans' urgent striving for it a misdirected (and futile) effort.[35]

Even Americans' assumption that happiness was worth pursuing because it was a desirable feeling could be wrong, according to at least one psychologist. In an article called "A Proposal to Classify Happiness as a Psychiatric Disorder" published in *Journal of Medical Ethics*,

Richard P. Bentall of Liverpool University argued that happiness was a "syndrome" not unlike other disorders like depression and schizophrenia. Happiness was "statistically abnormal, consists of a discrete cluster of symptoms, and is associated with a range of cognitive abnormalities," he wrote, thinking that the syndrome "reflects the abnormal functioning of the central nervous system." Luckily, happiness was "a relatively rare phenomenon," Bentall made clear, certainly a good thing given his conclusion that it qualified as a serious mental illness.[36]

When Will I Be Happy?

Bentall's controversial theory could have been considered welcome news given that the happiness syndrome had not reached epidemic levels in the United States. The latest numbers on international happiness had come in and, despite their concerted efforts, Americans were apparently not becoming happier people, at least on a comparative basis. Of thirty-nine countries surveyed, the United States now ranked twelfth in overall happiness, beaten out by much smaller and poorer nations such as Singapore and Luxembourg. Virtually all of Scandinavia—Denmark, Finland, Norway, Sweden, and Iceland—had also finished ahead of the United States, their low crime rate and absence of an underclass outweighing their chilly temperatures and long, dark winters. Scandinavians had an image of being a largely depressed, even suicidal people who drank large quantities of vodka to ease their angst, but the data suggested they were happier than supposedly chipper Americans.[37]

Americans' mediocre international showing with regard to happiness was also revealed by the ubiquity of psychotherapy in this country. Therapy of various sorts was more popular in the United States than anywhere else in the word, with much of it dedicated to the pursuit of happiness. "When will I be happy?" many a client asked his or her therapist, the question a difficult or impossible one to answer. Sigmund Freud had famously said that the most one could expect from therapy was "uncommon happiness," hardly the thing clients were willing to spend good money on. While certainly helpful in many cases, Western-style therapy often did not deliver the kind of happiness most clients were expecting to find, in part because it was rooted in our bipolar view of life. Get rid of the bad and replace it with the good, a fair number of therapists were telling their clients, sensible advice but a prescription that was difficult to achieve or sustain.[38]

Recognizing that traditional therapeutic methods often did not adequately address their clients' fervent wish to be happier, a growing number of American therapists were integrating Buddhist philosophy into their practice. "Buddhism holds the promise of more than just common unhappiness," stated Mark Epstein, one such therapist who was successfully combining Eastern and Western modalities of well-being. Those who practiced Buddhism "see the pursuit of happiness as our life goal," Epstein observed, and were prepared to apply "techniques of mental development to achieve it." Most Americans simply didn't understand what happiness was, Epstein believed, his experience showing that the key to achieving that state of being resided in what he called "inner development." Happiness had little to do with material comforts or sensory pleasures, he argued, and Americans' dream of having a completely problem-free life was plain unrealistic. For Epstein, happiness was "the ability to receive the pleasant without grasping and the unpleasant without condemning," a definition that most Americans would find completely incomprehensible.[39]

Even the prospect of all Americans becoming Zen Buddhists would apparently not make us an appreciably happier people, however. By the early 1990s, there was more evidence to suggest that an individual had less control over his or her happiness than we liked to believe due to our biological makeup. Two researchers at the University of Minnesota studying twins were making the case that a person's level of happiness was "pre-set" based on genetics, lending more support for the biological school of the field. One's relative state of happiness may increase on a good day and decrease on a bad one, the pair pointed out, but eventually it would return to its original "programmed" set point or "theromstat." Not all social scientists agreed with the theory, but it was clear that the winds of happiness were shifting toward genetics and away from environmental factors. Whatever the basis for happiness, the notion that there was likely some kind of scientific component was drawing more attention to the field. A growing number of academics from a variety of disciplines were now pursuing research in the field as it became increasingly apparent that there was much more to happiness than philosophical musings and pithy aphorisms.[40]

The idea that one's happiness was heavily determined at conception was of little interest to most ordinary Americans seeking more of it, however, and perhaps even less to the many self-professed experts in the bigger-than-ever industry dedicated to it. Over the past decade and a half, the happiness business had exploded, with all kinds of related products and services available to those wanting more ups than downs in their everyday lives. The broader personal development industry had ballooned too, driven by popular New Age thinking and charismatic superstars in the field like Deepak Chopra, James Redfield, M. Scott Peck, and John Bradshaw. Bookstores remained the commercial epicenter of self-help, but the Internet was fast becoming a one-stop-shop for quasi-spiritual advice, including that geared to happiness. Online self-publishing was taking off, allowing anyone with thoughts on happiness to become instantly seen as an authority on the subject. Recent titles included *Become Happy in Eight Minutes*, *The 10 Secrets of Abundant Happiness*, *The Alchemy of Happiness*, *14,000 Things to Be Happy About*, and, perhaps inevitably, *Animal Happiness*.[41]

Alongside such fluffier guidance, serious scholarly inquiry into the psychology of happiness was leading to some very valuable insights. In their article "Who Is Happy?" published in *Psychological Science* in May 1996, David Myers and Ed Diener offered what was arguably the most useful information on the subject published to date. Happiness was spread out evenly over the course of a lifetime, the psychologists argued, challenging the belief that it was higher in one's younger and older years than in middle age. Their research showed that black Americans were about as happy as white Americans, contesting the generally accepted idea that the former scored lower on happiness ratings. Gender, too, had little to do with happiness, according to Myers and Diener, and wealthier Americans were just marginally happier than their less well off neighbors. Most interesting, however, was the list of four personal traits that the pair found to be associated with high levels of happiness. The happiest Americans tended to be extroverted, to be optimistic, to have high self-esteem, and to feel like they were in control of their lives, their research showed, with the ability to adapt to change and be goal-oriented other key factors in the happiness equation.[42]

Dozens of perfectly reasonable theories regarding happiness were now in circulation, but few if any resonated more than Mihaly

Csikszentmihalyi's concept of "flow." The psychologist and University of Chicago professor struck a chord with his 1990 book, *Flow: The Psychology of Optimal Experience*, in which he argued that happiness was a function of being fully in the moment ("flow" continues to serve as a popular model for happiness; his book of that name was republished in 2008, and that same year he gave a TED talk on the subject). Csikszentmihalyi had been interested in happiness since his childhood in Hungary during World War II, with his hypothesis of flow gelling in the early 1970s. Most psychologists, especially those in the psychoanalytic school, tended to focus on the darker side of the human mind, making Csikszentmihali's more positive perspective rather revolutionary. That happiness was something that individuals could conjure by themselves was a refreshing alternative to the traditional psychological view that we were victims of our past as well to the ascending, biology-based view that we had to play with the hand we were dealt at birth. Flow also dovetailed nicely with Americans' can-do spirit (i.e., that anything was possible if one tried hard enough to achieve it).[43]

How exactly did Csikszentmihalyi's theory of flow relate to personal happiness? Happiness was a function of our degree of engagement with whatever we chose to do, he argued in *Flow* and his follow-up book *Finding Flow*, advising those seeking to be happier to become absorbed at work, during leisure time, and in relationships. Flow was "a state of effortless concentration and enjoyment," and the best thing about it was that it was of our own making. One usually lost track of time and felt like nothing else mattered during these exceptional moments, he explained, making it a worthy endeavor to try to integrate them into everyday life.[44] "Start doing more of what you love and less of what you hate," went his rather simple prescription to happiness, this "going with the flow" the most direct path to realizing greater happiness in life.[45]

It was easy to see how the roots of flow could be traced back to the elation one often feels when one is fully engaged in a creative pursuit. Csikszentmihalyi had done considerable research in the area of creativity, making it natural for him to find a link between happiness and creative people. Such folks loved what they did, he pointed out, the secret, if there was one, to being happy. If happiness was a "side effect" of making and discovering new things (scientists and inventors were also considered highly creative people), Csikszentmihalyi suggested, those wishing to be happier should consider enhancing their own creativity. What was perhaps most interesting about Csikszentmihalyi's view was that it challenged the popular belief that especially creative people tilted decidedly toward unhappiness, a by-product of their isolation, obsessive tendencies, and, often, cynical view of society. Rather, he argued, the most creative people were often the happiest, as it was they were who most able to escape the distractions of time and space through their art.[46]

An Extraordinarily Weak and Tenuous Relationship

Flow was all nice and good, but for many Americans it was money that remained the ideal perceived route to happiness. Studies to date had shown there to be little connection between relative wealth and happiness, but researchers, perhaps considering the findings difficult to believe, continued to investigate the area. What did the latest research reveal? "Money bears an extraordinarily weak and tenuous relationship to human happiness," declared Dan Seligman in *Forbes* in 1997 after reading a recent study published in the *Journal of Personality and Social Psychology*. This latest study lent greater support to the set point theory of happiness (i.e., that we all have a virtually unmovable baseline to which we continue to return following a positive or negative event in our lives). Warren Buffett, of all people, believed the theory was a valid one; the businessman felt he was just moderately happier than when he did not have billions of dollars in his bank account. The findings from this study echoed those published in the journal *Social Indicators Research* about a decade earlier, implying that becoming a millionaire or even billionaire was not the best route to raise one's level of happiness. Interestingly, Buffett believed that, based on his familiarity with other billionaires, having loads of money did not make one appreciably happier but rather reinforced one's existing character traits, that is, made an individual more of the person he or she already was.[47]

Despite such stories from people who were intimately familiar with the relationship between wealth and happiness, or the lack thereof, economists continued to investigate the topic. Why had average happiness levels not risen in the United States in decades despite the fact that individuals and the nation had gotten appreciably richer over the same period of time? they asked again, fully expecting that broad economic prosperity was the leading indicator of happiness. The most obvious answer was that what economists called "material aspirations" had run parallel with the rise in wealth, meaning that the more money one earned, the more one wanted to spend it. "Each step upward on the ladder of economic development merely stimulates new economic desires that lead the chase ever onward," posited Richard A. Easterlin, an economist at the University of Southern California, seeing no end for this spiral of wealth and wants. Easterlin's view appeared to contest Abraham Maslow's classic "hierarchy of needs," in which the psychologist theorized that people sought nonmaterial, higher goals once their basic needs were met. No such evolution took place, he argued, explaining why people didn't get happier as they became more financially secure.[48]

More research showed that money was far overrated as a factor of happiness. Much was being made about the need for lots of money when one retired, for example, but it was having friends rather than cash that was more likely to lead to older people's happiness, a 1998 University of Michigan study found. A social network was key for retirees' emotional well-being, according to the study that confirmed previous research, suggesting that Americans should not just build up their nest egg as they aged but develop a circle of people with whom they enjoyed spending time. "As baby boomers age, they probably should pay as much attention to their social lives as their financial portfolios," advised *USA Today Magazine* in reporting the findings that added to the mounting evidence that happiness was rooted in relationships with other people rather than how much money one had.[49] Some argued, however, that even more so than personal relationships (and much more than relative wealth), it was serving others in some way that led to true happiness. Regardless of age, those wishing to be happy should seek out opportunities to help those in need, experts in happiness were pointing out, an idea also backed up by research showing that it really was better to give than receive.[50]

The most recent news that more money did not equate with more happiness directly clashed with Americans' general beliefs regarding the economic and social rewards of upward mobility. Americans' average household income had risen dramatically over the past few decades, yet their individual and collective level of happiness hadn't nudged, raising the question of why most of us were working so hard to earn more money. Money clearly provided greater options, helped solve problems, and allowed a better quality of life, but it did not lead to more happiness, a frustrating thing for those believing that it would. Gender, age, and race mattered little in terms of the relationship, or lack thereof, between money and happiness, mirroring other studies showing that Americans of all types were remarkably similar when it came to happiness. Such qualitative research probing happiness was backed up by PET scans that revealed when a brain was happy or not. As such technology advanced, what was being called affective neuroscience was a growing field, one that was adding hard evidence to the generally anecdotal study of happiness.[51]

The rise of neuroscience within the study of happiness was an especially positive development given the haziness that still surrounded qualitative research in the field. Because happiness was, experts agreed, subjective in nature, it was logical that the measures used to determine how much or what kind of it individuals possessed were less than precise. In studies, researchers typically asked people about their *feelings* of happiness rather than happiness itself, firmly establishing the state of being as not just emotional but likely as a sensation that came and went. Questions about people's *thoughts* regarding their satisfaction in life were also usually posed, adding a more analytical component to happiness research. Measuring happiness by the frequency of positive or negative feelings was also common, a methodological technique that made sense but could hardly be considered scientific.[52]

Given the less than precise kind of research that had long informed the field, there was good reason to believe that Americans' claims regarding happiness were seriously overstated in polls and surveys. Those in the advice business were most likely to think that Americans were a far less happy people than they told pollsters. Dennis Wholey, author of *Are You Happy?* held that just 20 percent of us were actually happy based on his experience, while John Powell, author of *Happiness Is an Inside Job*, put the number at just 10 to 15 percent. National surveys of happiness used the crude descriptors of "very happy," "pretty happy," and "not too happy," with the majority of people understandably choosing the middle ground. The "very happy" and "pretty happy" people were then lumped together to arrive at the percentage of Americans who were "happy," something that made us feel good about ourselves and was media friendly but was fundamentally flawed in terms of research methodology.[53]

An Attitudinal Adjustment

If money didn't bring happiness, researchers continued to ask, what did? Life experience appeared to be a logical answer to the question, but this too often wasn't associated with happiness. Most of us probably know at least one person who is continually unhappy despite acquiring everything he or she had sought in life, and another individual who remains consistently upbeat despite experiencing a seemingly endless string of misfortunes (I call the former "malcontents"). "Like most people, I have an event-oriented, material notion of happiness," Dorothy Foltz-Gray wrote in *Health* in 1997, puzzled why getting the things one so desired did not result in a greater sense of well-being and why adversity did not make one just want to give up. While the workings of human happiness remained largely a mystery, Americans were more determined than ever to solve the puzzle, at least as it related to their own lives. Happiness self-help continued to grow, with books such as *Learned Optimism*, *Happier Starting Now*, and *You Can Get There From Here* adding to the literary genre.[54]

One writer argued that instead of chasing dollars, Americans should just get more sleep, as some research showed that having a good night's rest made an individual happier than having more money in his or her pockets.[55] Another study suggested that rather than being an enduring state of mind, happiness came in moments, making it unreasonable for people to expect to be happy all or even most of the time.[56] Other research showed that happiness could be simply a matter of avoiding pain, perhaps explaining why so many people had difficulty being happy.[57] A host of factors, including keeping busy, being healthy, having a network of friends, believing in God, or just getting older, were correlated with higher degrees of happiness, however, meaning there was likely more to the subject than just avoiding sadness and sorrow. Whatever the explanation, some practitioners of psychology had by the late 1990s begun offering clients "happiness therapy," a sign that Americans remained very interested in working on that part of their emotional set.

More research was showing that unless such books could lead to a wholesale personality change among readers, no amount of happiness advice was worth the time and money. Findings from a study conducted at the National Institute on Aging revealed that the happiness level of people hardly moved over the course of a decade regardless of what had taken place in their respective lives. "People's happiness levels had more to do with their personality traits than with things that happened to them," explained psychologist Robert R. McCrea, who headed up the study, suggesting that, in a nutshell, people were and would remain who they were. Good and bad things will inevitably happen in our lives, in other words, but it will be the brain's neural wiring that will primarily determine how happy or unhappy we will be. Most psychologists (perhaps only to keep their jobs) maintained that it was possible to increase one's happiness quotient a bit by doing things that one liked (or through intensive therapy), but it was becoming increasingly clear that genetics served as the guiding force of our personalities.[58]

Rather than solve the mystery of happiness, however, genetics only served to make the subject that much more perplexing. The more knowledge gained about happiness in general, in fact, the more baffling the subject seemed to be. Even defining the term beyond a "subjective state of well-being" remained as difficult as ever. Although virtually everybody wanted to be happy, few people could clearly articulate what would get them to that state of being, much less define the term itself (it's easier to know when one is unhappy versus happy, I'd say, and unhappiness is easier to describe than happiness). How does a person even know if he or she is happy, one could reasonably ask? How far along one was in reaching a certain goal was often the means of determining one's relative state of happiness, the more precise the goal the better. Many Americans, especially young people, looked to external measures such as wealth, fame, or power as a marker of happiness, but how much of any these was enough? The list of people who had achieved one or all of such markers and had had sad lives, often with tragic endings, was long, making one question if "success," broadly defined, was even correlated with happiness. More concerning, was actually finding happiness a bad thing in that it took away one's primary purpose to live, that individual having reached his or her ultimate goal?[59]

While brainier types pondered such existential issues, others were more interested in the practical side of happiness. There were many choices when it came to self-help or personal development, of course, but only one organization in the late 1990s focused exclusively on happiness: the Option Institute. Since 1983, people had come to the Option Institute campus in southwestern Massachusetts to find happiness, and were paying big bucks to do it (a one-week course at the institute cost

$1,175 in 1998, with four- and eight-week training sessions costing $4,500 and $8,500, respectively). "Beliefs and judgments which have created discomfort, distress, and self-defeating behaviors are gently uncovered, examined and discarded, leading to an increased sense of clarity, personal power and happiness," the company's literature read, incentive enough for thousands to have come to the institute over the years. Happiness was a choice, according to the institute's founder, Barry Kaufman, who had achieved tremendous success with his approach predicated on positive thinking and unconditional love (the source or level of one's unhappiness was immaterial to Kaufman; it was only making "an attitudinal adjustment," as he liked to say, that mattered). In addition to his institute (which still exists today, although its scope has broadened), Kaufman's books, audiotapes, and videotapes were readily available at larger bookstores, making him one of the superstars within self-help at the time.[60]

Other happiness gurus agreed that, while genetics played an important role, it was essentially up to individuals to decide to be happy or not. In their book *How We Choose to Be Happy*, Rick Foster and Greg Hicks made the case that some people are able to get the most out of their "God-given" abilities with regard to happiness, not unlike how overachievers exceed their natural talent in other arenas of life. Much of life may be beyond one's control, the pair of Bay-area leadership trainers conceded, but how one reacted to challenging situations was a matter of choice. "Happy people are unrelenting in their ability to find options and follow them," Foster said in a 1999 interview, convinced that the source of happiness was wholly internal. Personal achievements and even deep relationships were thus not avenues to happiness but the natural results of an individual's determination to be happy. "Love and success are the outcomes rather than the causes of happiness," Hicks observed, suggesting that many people were putting the cart before the horse in their attempts to be happier.[61] Many more such theories would be put forth in the new century, driven by a new narrative of happiness that gave Americans hope that their future would be a brighter one.

ARE YOU HAPPY YET?
2000–2009

Have a very active left prefrontal lobe day.
—George Mason University psychology professor
Todd Kashdan, 2007

In March 2003, *USA Weekend*, a Sunday supplement included in about six hundred newspapers across the country, announced it had big news. The publication had found who it called "The Happiest Man in America," naming a forty-five-year-old Virginia Beach, Virginia, stockholder as the winner of its nationwide search. J. P. "Gus" Godsey had beat out the likes of President Bush, Bill Gates, Tom Cruise, and Bruce Springsteen, a reporter informed readers, with editors of *USA Weekend* using "a combination of science, sleuthing and surveys" to make their choice. Godsey had endured a series of interviews and psychological tests as part of the selection process, but the man felt it was well worth it. "It's real cool," the big-smiling, fast-talking Godsey told the media, with an appearance on ABC's *Good Morning America* already scheduled and Regis, Oprah, and Letterman also interested. Godsey did volunteer work and was deeply involved in the Virginia Beach community, but it was his remarkable amiability and extremely positive attitude toward life that pushed him over the top. "We wake up every morning full of choices and your state of happiness is something you can do every single day," the happiest man in America observed, promising not to get caught up in all the hype.[1]

Many Americans could only wish for Godsey's upbeat take on life and cheery disposition that even perfect strangers could immediately detect. It was a new century and new millennium, but most Americans were waking up and going to sleep in a much different mood than that of the happiest man in the nation. Midlife crises were wreaking havoc with the happiness of aging baby boomers, for one thing, and it was not helpful to learn that Iceland, of all places, was populated with much happier citizens than the United States.[2] Worse news, perhaps, were new findings suggesting that ignorance really was bliss; more knowledge was correlated with less happiness, according to the study, implying that an educated public was an unhappy public.[3] "Are you happy yet?" Andrew Delbanco asked in the *New York Times Sunday Magazine* in May 2000, the answer for most Americans likely *no*.[4] Was it was even possible for Americans to be happy people, one had to ask, or was broad happiness simply not part of our national character?

Happy Days Are Here Again

With such a question being posed, theories regarding the dynamics of happiness and treatments intended to boost it flourished in the early 2000s. One theory postulated that individuals have different selves or personalities, making it incumbent on each person to find and "occupy" the happiest one. This idea went further by asserting that this character was the "real" you, and that one thus had to eradicate the less happy pretenders.[5] A twist on this theory was that there have been happy and less than happy times in each person's life, and that individuals should rediscover the happiest period and occupy that self.[6] If such psychological machinations didn't work, there was good old medication; antidepressants had been around for some time, of course, but now Big Pharma was offering "anti-unhappiness" drugs to consumers or repositioning SSRIs as such.[7]

Whether it was due to new century and new millennium jitters, post-9/11 anxieties, or something else, there seemed to be no shortage of cures for Americans seeking greater happiness in the early 2000s. A more interesting one conceded that long-term happiness was for some a lost cause; such individuals should focus only on the present, this theory went, and let the future take care of itself.[8] This idea fit in well with the "now" culture that was emerging at the time (i.e., consumers' interest in products and services that could be had instantly). An alternative was to simply get a pooch; dog therapy was known to make many people with serious medical conditions feel better, suggesting that having an animal companion could alleviate unhappiness as well.[9] Widespread, perhaps epidemic levels of unhappiness among Americans were in part a function of people feeling like they were judged by how happy they were or weren't. Happiness was perhaps more than ever recognized as a form of social status, with individuals effectively ranked by others along a happy-or-unhappy scale just as they might by income or net worth.[10]

Naturally, happiness continued to be in vogue within the psychological community, part of professionals' decades long deemphasis on the darker goings-on of the human mind. "Happy days are here again as American psychology shifts its focus from what is wrong with humans to what is right," declared Alison Stein Wellner and David Adox in *Psychology Today* in 2000 as the "positive psychology" movement gained further steam. Martin Seligman, a former president of the American Psychological Association and a professor at the University of Pennsylvania, was one of the key figures in the field's new emphasis on people's emotional strengths versus their perceived weaknesses. Rather than identify a problem and then try to correct it—the typical modus operandi of psychology and psychiatry since Sigmund Freud began publishing his work a century ago—more practitioners were placing greater value on the many positive aspects of personality. Seligman was even being called by some in psychological circles "the Freud of the twentieth century," a sign of how pronounced this shift was within the field of mental health.[11]

The redirection of psychology in the United States was just one of a host of signs that happiness was gaining ever more cultural currency in the country. "The happiness business is booming in America," pronounced Delbanco that same year, adding that "it seems to have entered a new phase of hype and strain." Delbanco argued that the greater intensity of happiness had much to do with its continued shift to a privately defined and pursued concept. For the first half or so of American history, he observed, happiness had generally resided in the public domain due to the heavy value placed on social and communal values. The nation's deeply religious roots also discouraged personal notions of happiness, with the emotion seen as something to be experienced more in the afterlife versus this one. The ascent of free-market capitalism after the Civil War put an end to this public, postponed version of happiness, however, with self-interests guiding not just one's financial orientation but one's desired emotional state as well.[12]

Despite all the resources being devoted to it, the much-hyped, privatized expression of happiness in the United States in the early twenty-first century had yet to make Americans a measurably happier people. The number of Americans who described themselves as happy had not budged since World War II, begging the question of whether the great amounts of effort and money being spent were worth it. Keeping one's perspective and having the courage to make changes in one's life when things were going less than well were linked to happiness, psychologists were finding, but were such common sense insights of any value? While psychologists were claiming to be uncovering some of the mysteries of happiness, and asserting that for some it could perhaps be a learned or cultivated trait, there was no evidence that Americans were any happier than during Freud's heyday. "Positive psychology" certainly sounded like a healthier way to view an individual's personality profile, but was it making any difference in terms of Americans' actual emotional well-being? The answer appeared to be *no*, with happiness in America as elusive as ever.[13]

Although positive psychology was a very media-friendly idea and "positivism" in any capacity was difficult to make a case against, the so-called revolution in happiness appeared to be more about money. Virtually everyone wanted more happiness in their life, making the marketing of it too irresistible for companies in a wide range of industries and product categories. "Everyone's selling happiness these days," noted Robert Epstein, editor in chief of *Psychology Today*, in 2001, naming "drug dealers, pharmaceutical companies, Hollywood producers, toy companies, self-help gurus, and the Disney Company" as some of those getting in on the action. Epstein had doubts that Americans' stepped up pursuit of happiness would lead to much, however, thinking in fact that it could be doing more damage than good. "The quest for happiness is probably overrated and is, ironically, the cause of much unhappiness," he continued, agreeing with many critics of the past who held that chasing the emotion rarely if ever resulted in catching it. "Demanding happiness, even desiring it, can keep it out of reach," Epstein concluded, seeing this latest round of happiness-mania as good for business but scientifically questionable.[14]

As usual, happiness represented a big chunk of self-help and how-to literature. *The Art of Happiness*, coauthored by the Dalai Lama, was still selling briskly after its initial release in 1998, good reason for other publishers to try to repeat its success.[15] Steven Reiss's *Who Am I?* argued that there were no less than sixteen "basic desires that motivate our happiness and define our personalities," for example, with readers encouraged to rate themselves on those dimensions as the first step in becoming a happier person.[16] Martin Seligman, meanwhile, was capitalizing on the current buzz over positive psychology with *Authentic Happiness*, a follow-up to his *Learned Optimism* published a dozen years earlier. In his new book, Seligman offered up nuggets like "keep your illusions" and "turn work into play" as the means for readers to find "lasting fulfillment."[17]

Scholarly research in the field complemented such popular forays into happiness self-help. Ed Diener, who was sometimes called "the guru of American happiness studies" or more simply "Dr. Happiness," was still exploring the subject at his "happiness lab" at the University of Illinois. New findings confirmed the personal and social value of happiness. Happy people were healthier, more creative, and more productive than unhappy people, Diener (now along with his wife and three of his children) had found, part of the reason being that the former were willing to search for new solutions to problems. Diener, editor of the *Journal of Happiness Studies*, was one of about one hundred academics pursuing happiness research in the early 2000s, and the first textbook in the field, *Well-Being: The Foundations of Hedonistic Psychology*, had recently been published (with Diener as one of the coauthors). As a college student at Fresno State, Diener was told by his advisor that studying happiness was "flaky" and that it would "ruin your career," but history had proven otherwise as what was being billed as an entirely new branch of psychology grew and grew.[18]

The Futile Pursuit of Happiness

Indeed, Americans could choose from a plethora of books promising to make readers happier people in the new century. *Wholly Joy: Being Happy in an Unhappy World*, *The Lazy Person's Guide to Happiness*,

The Buddhist Eight Steps to Happiness, and *I'd Rather Laugh: How to Be Happy Even When Life Has Other Plans for You* were just a few recently published books whose authors were clearly trying to capitalize on the apparent spike of interest in happiness. The tragic event of 9/11 and the chaos that followed perhaps played a role in Americans' more pronounced searching for happiness in the early 2000s. Unfortunately, few of these books offered any real long-term value for readers, in part because they lacked an empirical foundation. Many if not most of the authors of such books had no psychological or psychiatric training, and little of what they produced was based on reliable research. Not surprisingly, then, critics found the genre as a whole inconsistent, superficial, and overly reliant on warm and fuzzy, Oprahesque philosophy.[19]

To be fair, the sketchy nature of happiness self-help was not entirely writers' fault. Although many in the media had taken to calling it a science, happiness remained heavily (and perhaps entirely) qualitative and subjective in nature. It was up to each individual to describe his or her own state of happiness or unhappiness, with no reliable means to quantify or accurately measure it. Just as the medical community was primarily equipped to address physical health problems, mental health professionals tended to focus on "negative" emotions, particularly depression. More bluntly, there was more money to be made by researchers in finding potential solutions to psychological problems than in gaining new insights into positive emotions like happiness. With their solid credentials, Diener and Seligman were more the exception than the rule, as was Dan Baker, a psychologist and head of the Life Enhancement Program at Canyon Ranch in Tucson, Arizona. Baker, author of *What Happy People Know*, was of the happiness-can-be-managed-and-controlled school of thought, defining the skill as "the ability to practice appreciation or love."[20]

Not everyone, however, was convinced that an individual could shape his or her level of happiness as one could improve physical health by taking certain steps. In an article tellingly titled "The Futile Pursuit of Happiness" for the *New York Times Sunday Magazine*, Jon Gertner challenged the new wave of thinking that greater degrees of the emotion could be developed like bigger abs. The main problem was that most people were not very good at predicting what would make them happy, an elite group of researchers was coming to believe based on a number of empirically sound studies. Daniel Gilbert of Harvard, Tim Wilson of the University of Virginia, George Loewenstein of Carnegie-Mellon, and Daniel Kahneman of Princeton were concluding that Americans' determined efforts to find happiness were misguided as what they believed would turn them into permanently happy people turned out to be not so. In a nutshell, it was simply impossible for the majority of individuals to map out a master plan for enhanced happiness and then execute it, they agreed, as the human mind just didn't work that way.[21]

Advancements in neuroscience and the completion of the Human Genome Project in 2003 each had a direct effect on the trajectory of happiness in America. Each person did indeed have what could be considered a happiness gene, scientists were concluding, making one's relative state of happiness or unhappiness more a matter of biology than psychology. MRI scans plainly revealed when a person was happy, with that part of his or her brain lighting up like a Christmas tree. Altering one's happiness gene could one day be possible, more scientists were beginning to think, with such an approach to be far more effective than all the how-tos grounded in some kind of attitudinal or behavioral modification put together.[22] Until that point, however, the less than happy had to continue to rely more on psychological, philosophical, or spiritual techniques to reconfigure their happiness equation. Zen Buddhism was becoming an increasingly popular choice in the nation's spiritual marketplace, with its set of beliefs well suited for seeing the glass half full versus half empty ("Calm is the new happiness," some were beginning to say).[23]

While both Loewenstein and Kahneman crossed the lines of psychology and economics in their work, those two fields were generally divided in terms of how they viewed individuals' capacity for happiness. As genetics became seen as playing a major role in determining one's emotional framework, more psychologists were embracing the set point theory of happiness. Significant life events, good or bad, would likely move one's level of happiness up or down for a certain amount of time, but eventually it would stabilize to its previous and normal degree. Through "hedonic adaptation," people adapted or adjusted to life situations, believers in the theory held, as a kind of survival mechanism went into effect. If this was true, the implication was that there was little people could do in terms of aspiring to become consistently happier, and that the huge industry dedicated to it was a giant sham. As well, the set point theory suggested that governmental efforts to improve citizens' social and economic status were pointless, as greater personal prosperity would not make people happier for an extended period of time.[24]

Most economists, however, were trained to think much differently. Wealth made a difference in terms of both individual and national happiness, they believed, making it vital that people strive to make more money and for governments to try to improve the economic lot of its citizens. "The implication is that one can improve one's happiness by getting more money, and that public policy measures aimed at increasing the income of society as a whole will increase well-being," as Richard A. Easterlin described it in *Daedulus* in 2004. Interestingly, Easterlin, an economist at the University of Southern California, rejected both the set point theory of psychology and the wealth-based view of economics, choosing instead a perspective grounded in the autonomy of the self. Happiness was a function of "the things that occupy most people's everyday lives, and are somewhat within their control," he wrote, thinking that the normal ups and downs of life trumped both biology and bureaucracy in terms of making one either happy or unhappy.[25]

Like most of his colleagues, Robert H. Frank, an economist at Cornell, bought into the money-can-buy-some-degree theory of happiness, but put a twist on it. It was what one actually purchased that made a difference regarding the question of whether money could buy happiness, he believed, drawing a distinction between conspicuous consumption and inconspicuous consumption. Frank agreed with the research showing that spending money on material goods, even expensive items like a house or car, did not result in any long-term, appreciable difference in a consumer's level of happiness. But buying what Frank called "inconspicuous goods," such as using an express lane in order to shorten a long commute so that one could spend more time doing what one wanted to do, could indeed make someone happier, he proposed. Spending money to improve one's quality of life made sense for seekers of happiness, in other words, while simply adding another thing or experience to one's consumer portfolio would not yield any significant results. The marketplace could be a source of happiness, Frank believed, but Americans needed to shift their purchase decision making away from the mere collection of goods to those things that made a meaningful difference in their lives.[26]

The Very Motion of Our Life

While economists continued to make the case that money did matter when it came to happiness, psychologists specializing in the area took time to point out how much progress had been made in their field. New thinking and better research methodologies had turned the study of happiness into a legitimate science, they claimed, making it no longer the exclusive province of philosophy and religion. It was true that much more was known about the social and biological factors that influenced happiness, and debunking myths that had long been associated with the emotion was another major leap that had been made in recent years. "By employing testable hypotheses, longitudinal designs, controlled experiential studies, and multiple measurement methods, researchers have been able to explain aspects of subjective well-being more definitively than the less formal approaches common in the past were equipped to," wrote Diener along with two colleagues at Illinois (one of them his son, who was following in his dad's academic footsteps).[27]

While such scientific slicing and dicing of happiness was adding some much-needed credibility to the field, many Americans were looking to a Buddhist monk to find it. Since the publication of his book, the Dalai Lama had achieved rock-star status, speaking to crowds at venues usually headlined by wealthy musicians with much different ideas regarding the route to happiness. The exiled leader of Tibet and Nobel Prize winner (whose given name at birth was Lhamo Dhondup) was considered by some to be "the high priest of happiness," and millions of Westerners (including a fair share of psychologists) were very interested in what the man had to say on the matter. Rather than tell Westerners to pursue an ascetic life, as what one might have expected from a monk, His Holiness the Dalai Lama, the 14th manifestation of the Buddha of Compassion, was positively gung-ho on happiness. The purpose of life was to "seek happiness," he told readers in his book, which was a ninety-seven-week bestseller, going even further by asserting that "the very motion of our life is toward happiness."[28]

It was clear that the Dalai Lama was able to present "the art of happiness" in a more compelling way than wonky academics or touchy-feely self-helpers. "No one has promoted the gospel of cultivated happiness more exuberantly than the Dalai Lama," wrote Chip Brown for *Smithsonian* in 2004, thinking that the monk was expressing the latest scientific findings from the field but through the lens of Buddhism. One could alter one's emotions in a positive manner, His Holiness told rapt audiences, and a trained mind could tell the brain what to think. The Dalai Lama was in fact trying to bridge the gap between Eastern religion and Western science, finding the common pursuit of happiness to be the ideal means to do just that. "You can find more articulate and intellectually stimulating summations of the Buddhist path to happiness than *The Art of Happiness*, but you won't find an author who embodies the message as completely," Brown observed, thinking the man's Tibetan moniker of "Kundun" (the presence) was well deserved.[29]

The wild popularity of the Dalai Lama and his compassion-based happiness were clear signs that many Americans were searching for something in life they had yet to find. As usual, polls did not seem to be a reliable indicator of genuine happiness in the country; the gap between what Americans told researchers and how they actually felt was as large as ever. In a 2005 survey conducted by *Time* magazine, 78 percent of Americans said they felt happy most or all of the time, but reality suggested otherwise. "Beneath the national contentment there's evidence of a creeping dissatisfaction," the editor of that magazine told readers by way of introducing a special issue dedicated to happiness. Americans were collectively more prosperous than they had ever been, but many were in therapy, taking antidepressants, getting divorced, experiencing midlife crises, and buying self-help books in bulk. Were Americans a generally happy people or not? one had to ask, the answer as unclear as ever.[30]

Given the strides that were being made in understanding human happiness, one would think that Americans were becoming individually and collectively happier. That simply wasn't the case, however; if anything, the number of happy Americans was getting lower versus higher (going back decades, the number of Americans claiming to be happy most or all of the time was 80 to 90 percent). Happiness was flaunted as being in the midst of a scientific revolution not unlike that experienced by biology or chemistry hundreds of years ago, but none of these findings appeared to be helping Americans in any appreciable way. It was certainly interesting to learn of "the biology of joy" and "the paths to pleasure," as *Time* presented certain scientific breakthroughs in happiness, but how was anyone actually benefitting from such research?[31] It was admittedly early in the game, but translating findings into action-able results was a leap that had yet to be made, and perhaps would never be made.

The inability to help those people seeking greater happiness was not for lack of trying. Linda Carstensen, a professor of psychology at Stanford, was studying the relationship between happiness and aging, and finding that older people were not at all the grouches they were believed to be. She and her team were also analyzing the techniques of Buddhist meditators in order to see if there was anything less Zen types could learn from them. Psychologist Richard Davidson at the University of Wisconsin was also examining the effect of meditation on the brain, finding that the palpable happiness of Buddhist monks was biologically based. Activity in their left prefrontal cortex was much higher than that in their right—the latter being responsible for negative emotions—a result of the apparent ability of meditation to "reshape" the brain. Mindfulness, the increasingly popular idea that focusing on the present was emotionally beneficial, could thus be a means to greater happiness, some believed, a good example of the potential applications of research in the field.[32]

Research into happiness in the first decade of the twenty-first century drifted decidedly toward the notion that the trouble with finding it was somehow a fault of or deficiency in the mind. Kaja Perina, now the editor of *Psychology Today*, concluded that happiness just did not come naturally to humans, a refreshing observation that challenged Americans' expectation that most of us should be happy most of the time. Memories of what we believed had made us happy at the time were incorrect, she felt after reviewing the essays for an issue in that magazine, leading us down wrong paths when searching for future happiness. "We're error-prone animals," she wrote in 2005, thinking that all of us were somehow "deluded about our happiest moments." Advances in neuroscience and behavioral decision theory were showing that our minds often did not operate in the rational, logical way we liked to believe, implying that emotions like happiness did not follow a straight, linear path. "Happiness, it seems, is a matter of instinct, not intellect," Perina observed, making it no wonder that the subject remained largely a mystery despite scientists' best efforts to understand it.[33]

An Active Embracing of the World

In fact, perhaps the most significant thing recently learned about human happiness was that people had relatively little control over it. People could determine only about 10 to 15 percent of their happiness quotient, more researchers were coming to believe, with genetics and ingrained personality traits having far more sway than previously thought. One would think that how well (or unwell) things were going for an individual was the chief determinant of that person's level of happiness, but that did not seem to be the case. This explained the fleeting nature of happiness, why having more money typically did not make people any happier, and why the self-help industry dedicated to it remained so robust despite falling well short of its promises. "Happiness is stubborn, difficult to find, and difficult to augment," wrote Kathleen McGowan for *Psychology Today*, with only so much we could do to increase the amount of it in our lives.[34]

Although it appeared that people could move their happiness needle just 10 to 15 percent, much advice continued to be doled out if only to take comfort that we had some control over our emotions. Americans were deeply rooted in the values of change, progress, and improvement, after all, making it a depressing thought to believe that becoming a happier person was a hopeless pursuit. Feeling good about oneself, not taking things so seriously, spending time with friends, finding time to have fun, and volunteering were some ways to maximize one's happiness potential, McGowan advised, with not just money but beauty, youth, education, and intelligence far overrated when it came to that effort.[35] Sonja Lyubomirsky, a University of California–Riverside psychologist, added counting your blessings and practicing acts of kindness to the list, finding in her research that embracing such values as thankfulness, gratitude, and forgiveness were common to happy people.[36]

While such advice made sense and it certainly couldn't hurt to have more thankful, grateful, and forgiving people around, a more reliable path to happiness was to be hardwired for it by having an active left prefrontal cortex. In his research at the University of Wisconsin, Richard Davidson had found that rather than being the abstruse emotion described by philosophers for centuries, happiness was a very real condition of the brain. Not only that, he learned, but feelings of happiness could be created with a few electrodes attached to one's noggin, additional evidence that the emotion was rooted more in biology than psychology. Of course, chemistry also played a major role in determining one's level of happiness; dopamine and endorphins were the two brain chemicals primarily responsible for promoting feelings of pleasure and joy.[37] Being happy had all kinds of positive effects upon a person's physical health, Davidson and others had also found, further establishing the link between body and mind.[38]

While defining happiness in a meaningful way remained difficult at best (Davidson defined it as a "kind of a placeholder for a constellation of positive emotional states"), there was no doubt that researchers were gaining a much better understanding of its neurological goings-on. The good news for those whose left prefrontal cortexes were less than busy was that the brain was a highly plastic thing, meaning that it could be rewired over time and with considerable effort (explaining Buddhist monks' overtly happy states of being gained through years of deep meditation). From a historical view, such findings represented a giant leap in our knowledge of the workings of happiness, but Davidson admitted there was much more work to be done. Happiness was "associated with an active embracing of the world," he explained, "but its precise characteristics and boundaries have really yet to be seriously characterized in scientific research."[39]

While researchers like Davidson probed the brain to find answers to why some people were happier than others, those on the "softer" side of the psychological fence focused more on behavioral and environmental factors. Members of this group were clearly unwilling to concede that happiness was primarily a biological function that one had relatively little control over. At Harvard University, for example, psychologist Tal Ben-Shahar's course on how to be happy was the most popular on campus, reassuring its 850 enrollees that happiness could be a learned skill. "When you give yourself permission to be human," Ben-Shahar lectured, "you are more likely to open yourself up to positive emotions." For positive psychologists like he, happiness resided as much in conscious decisions like accepting one's faults as in how jumpy one's left cortex happened to be. There might be some kind of set point or genetic regulator of happiness and other emotions, positivists conceded, but everyone could agree that moods often fluctuated wildly based on situation and circumstance. As well, while there was considerable evidence to support the set point theory, the point could shift up (or down) over an extended period of time, one study showed, more reason for those seeking greater happiness in their lives to remain hopeful.[40]

Those believing that environmental factors played a significant role in determining one's level of happiness placed considerable value on where one chose (or was forced) to live. Now at Portland State, Robert Biswas-Diener had become the go-to person in the geography of happiness, ranking cities and nations along that dimension on a scale of one to seven. Latin Americans scored highly on Biswas-Diener's index of subjective well-being, which was consistent with other such studies, while Asians fell toward the bottom of the list, this too not a surprise given previous rankings. Outlook on life was one of the key differences between people on opposite sides of the world, according to Biswas-Diener, the former tending to focus on the positive and the latter on the negative. American college students tied for eighth place in happiness with their Slovenian counterparts, rankings that were taken in the United States as not very good news but was cause for celebration in Slovenia.[41]

Biswas-Diener wasn't the only one plumbing the geography of happiness, however. Adrian White of the University of Leicester in the UK had created a World Map of Happiness as a tool to help elected officials know if happiness was heading north or south in their respective countries, and then to tweak social programs accordingly. Aggregating data from UNESCO, the CIA, the World Health Organization, and other sources, White found that health, wealth, and opportunities for education were the most important indicators of a nation's level of happiness. Denmark, Switzerland, and Austria topped the list of this study that ranked 178 countries, with the Democratic Republic of the Congo, Zimbabwe, and Burundi finishing last. The United States ranked twenty-third, again hardly something that Americans found reassuring regarding the possibilities to find the happiness they were seeking.[42]

The High Price of Materialism

White's study was well received by economists unwilling to give up on the idea that wealth was tied to both national and individual happiness. Many critics (in wealthier countries, it should be said) roundly dismissed money as a factor in generating high degrees of happiness, but a glance at the winners and losers of the World Map of Happiness suggested that wealth did indeed matter (wealth was directly related to health and opportunities for education, compounding its potential effect on happiness).[43] Why then had happiness levels in the United States remained essentially frozen since the 1950s despite the nation's nothing-less-than-phenomenal economic strides, people asked again, whether that growth was measured by inflation-adjusted income or the average square footage of a newly constructed house? "Money jangles in our wallets and purses as never before, but we are basically no happier for it," wrote Gregg Easterbrook for *Time*, with many an American hearing stories from their grandparents about how happy they were during the Great Depression despite being as poor as dirt.[44]

The best answer to the oft-asked question "Does money buy happiness?" was "Only up to a point." Despite grandma's fond memories of the 1930s, being poor was strongly correlated with unhappiness, making it not surprising that relatively wealthy Danes were rated as considerably happier than poverty-stricken Burundians. Making money was for the most part an individual activity while the happier moments in life tended to derive from social experiences, however, something that perhaps put a cap on happiness levels in wealthier countries. In the United States, making and spending money was often used as a shortcut to happiness, with many Americans learning the hard way that taking a purely economic route led to a dead end. "Reference anxiety," the disturbing feeling that one had less than others (even if one had a lot), also took the wind out of happiness for many. The rich had pulled further away from the middle-class pack over the last few decades (and the superrich from the rich), making our keep-up-with-the-Joneses society not ideal in terms of seeding happiness for a large number of people.[45]

That money and happiness did not follow parallel paths resided in the simple fact that humans didn't always think or behave logically. More was not necessarily more and less not necessarily less, a source of frustration for economists taught otherwise. "The relationship between money and happiness, it would appear, is more complicated than the romantic entanglements of any Desperate Housewife," wrote David Futrelle for *Money* in 2006, offering some much-needed clarity on the matter. The amount of money that people think would make them happy, should they be able to get it, was a moving target, Futrelle explained, with the bar continually raised after reaching one's goal. Most people thus never reached a point of monetary satisfaction, it could safely be said based on psychologists' research, reason for those engaged in a wealth-based pursuit of happiness to feel like they were always falling short.[46]

While certainly good for the economy and company shareholders, the endless cycle of consumerism was a black hole for those looking to the marketplace to find happiness. Owning something just didn't typically result in the degree of pleasure that had been anticipated by the buyer, the fulfillment to be gained greater in one's imagination than in reality. With always something newer and shinier to be had, it was easy to become disenchanted with what one possessed, no matter how wonderful that thing looked in the store or online. Experiences were likely to bring longer-lasting happiness than things in part because humans were very good at reconstructing what had actually taken place. People generally edited out the bad stuff and left in the good, creating an experience that could be filed away as a happy memory.[47]

While the life span of most experiences was shorter than that of most things in the real world (say, spending a few days at Disneyworld versus owning a new Lexus for a few years), it was the former that tended to endure in one's memory and contribute more to one's happiness. Leaf Van Boven of the University of Colorado at Boulder was exploring the emotional impact of experiences versus things, and finding that most Americans seeking happiness were investing much too heavily in possessions. Not only were experiences capable of living forever in one's mind, but they tended to be social, again something that was strongly correlated with happiness. Van Boven had also found that the feeling of achievement and accomplishment that often came with more challenging experiences provided a halo of happiness that could never result from the purchase of a material object. As well, one was far more likely to receive admiration from others for completing a triathlon or trekking in Nepal than buying the newest iPhone, a jolt of social status that was also known to deliver a healthy dose of happiness. The fact that having such experiences required more time than acquiring a thing made many Americans go the materialistic route, however, their hard-earned money going largely for naught in terms of chasing happiness.[48]

With research showing that owning more stuff was unlikely to offer the emotional rewards people were expecting, experts advised Americans to look to experiences versus things when shopping for happiness.

"The pursuit of money and the pursuit of happiness often get equated, especially in our success-addled culture," noted Jean Chatzey in *Money* in 2007, emphasizing that the bigger bang for the buck resided in doing versus having things. Books such as Daniel Gilbert's *Stumbling on Happiness*, Stefan Klein's *The Science of Happiness*, and Tim Kasser's *The High Price of Materialism* were all making the case that maximizing one's limited resources required avoiding the seduction of the marketplace. Much happiness could be found in the normalcy of everyday life, the anticipation of an upcoming trip, doing something new, getting involved in a cause, and finding a job that one loved, Chatzky told readers, good news for those thinking that only being able to afford that 55" high-definition plasma TV would make them happy.[49]

Enough Already

In addition to pointing out likely sources of happiness, steps were being taken to address Americans' fundamental lack of education in the subject. Positive psychology was taking the country's college and university system by storm, with more than two hundred schools offering classes with titles like "The Science of Well-Being." It was clear that many educators had embraced the movement that Martin Seligman had been credited with founding a decade or so ago, fully aware that students wondering what they should do in life would enroll in such courses in droves. A good number of "life coaches"—consultants who help guide clients along their personal and/or professional path—had also become smitten with the concept of positive psychology, not surprisingly, as it served as a handy theoretical device to motivate people to, as it was often said, follow their bliss. Thinking every night of the good things that happened that day, focusing on one's strengths, and thanking those who made a difference in one's life were all practices positive psychologists recommended to those looking for greater happiness.[50]

With positive psychology beginning to creep into the curricula of more progressive high schools, it was not surprising to see a backlash against happiness-mania emerge. "Enough already," declared Sharon Begley in *Newsweek* in 2008, thinking Americans' 232-year pursuit of happiness had spun out of control. Teenagers feeling down after a breakup with their boyfriend or girlfriend were being advised by adults to get counseling or get a prescription for the antidepression drug Zoloft as ways to reboot their level of happiness, and grievers were sometimes told it was time to "move on" after the loss of a loved one. The reaction to the nation's happiness-at-any-cost ethos had much to do with the ascending value being placed on the role of sadness in everyday life. Most experts on happiness had actually always recognized the importance for people to occasionally be sad, seeing it as an entirely normal emotion. It was also not unusual for the happiest people to report deep bouts of unhappiness, reason to conclude that the emotions were not oppositional and operated on different spectrums.[51]

With the publication of Jerome Wakefield's and Allan Horwitz's *The Loss of Sadness: How Psychiatry Transformed Normal Sorrow Into Depressive Disorder* and Eric G. Wilson's *Against Happiness: In Praise of Melancholy*, however, the backlash against Americans' obsession with happiness that had probably been simmering for years bubbled over. Each book served as a wake-up call for those maintaining that happiness was at the top of the emotional heap, and that lacking it for a period of time, even for a good reason, signaled an unnatural and possibly dangerous mental condition. Sadness occupied a valuable place in people's lives and in society as a whole, more people were coming to believe, and at the same time were beginning to think that happiness was drastically overemphasized in Western culture. Many were also coming to resent the pressure being put on them to be happy, sensing the presence of a kind of emotional police constantly on the lookout for "unhealthy" signs of sadness.[52]

With an anti-happiness movement seemingly in the works, Begley proposed that a tipping point in happiness may have been reached. "Look carefully, and what you are seeing now may be the end of the drive for ever-greater heights of happiness," she wrote, as a growing number of people started to rebel against the governing of their psyches. Even Ed Diener, the reigning king of happiness research, appeared to be wondering if positive psychology had pushed the drive for the "subjective state of well-being" too far. He and his son Robert had written a new book, *Happiness: Unlocking the Mysteries of Psychological Wealth*, which supported the idea that too many parties with their own (profit-making) agendas had gotten into the happiness game. Happiness-inducing "ozone enemas" were now being sold, clear evidence that the amount of money to be made by selling the emotion was too tempting for disreputable marketers to leave on the table.[53]

More than that, however, Diener and his colleagues had found that generally happy people tended to be more successful than extremely happy people, a function of the former being more motivated than the latter to achieve great things in life. Why then urge to maximize the emotion if 8s (on a happiness scale of 1 to 10) were doing better than 10s? they reasonably asked. Those in a less than cheery mood were also inclined to be analytical, critical, and innovative, they pointed out, making excessive amounts of happiness a deterrent for intellectually rigorous and creative thinking. Finally, and perhaps most important, sadness (but not depression) was part of life's rich pageant, Wilson argued in his book, with those committed to making it go away missing out on a key dimension of the human experience. Being melancholy encouraged "a turbulence of heart that results in an active questioning of the status quo, a perpetual longing to create new ways of being and seeing," Wilson poetically wrote, with figures like Lincoln, Beethoven, Van Gogh, and other glum geniuses able to attest to that.[54]

Along with a budding anti-happiness movement came a pushback against the set point theory of happiness and, more broadly, against the theory that genetics essentially dictated how happy or unhappy we would be. In 2008, Sonja Lyubomirsky, the University of California–Riverside professor, suggested that, based on her research with twins, no less than 40 percent of happiness was controllable, a much higher percentage than the 10 to 15 percent previously thought. Genetics accounted for 50 percent and the remaining 10 percent had to do with life circumstances—if true, good news for those assuming they were victims to their less-than-happy genes. Going further, Lyubomirsky offered readers tips that came out of her findings to increase their own levels of happiness. Avoid dwelling on negative situations, resist pessimism, revel in life's pleasures, and nurture optimism, she recommended, believing that such techniques were not just happiness boosters but could help make one's mind more predisposed toward thinking positive thoughts.[55]

If happiness really could be developed as Lyubomirsky and the positive psychologists maintained, the implications for society were huge. Could moods be contagious? some public health experts were beginning to wonder, intrigued by the possibility that happiness could spread to others like a germ. "Can you catch a case of happy?" asked Alice Park in *Time* in 2008 in reporting the rather sudden interest in virus-like behavior (social media, the ability for a video to "go viral," and phenomena like flash mobs were no doubt fueling such interest). As well, Nicholas Christakis, a Harvard social scientist, and James Fowler, a political science professor at the University of California at San Diego, had just created a buzz by proclaiming that an individual's happiness can influence those of a group of people up to three degrees of separation away. Even total strangers could thus be infected by a person's happiness, the pair's research suggested, with Christakis making the case that society functioned as a kind of super-organism and had a collective identity. "If you're feeling happy, you can thank your friends," Park observed, posing the intriguing notion that a "happiness effect" was influencing each of us in ways that we were not aware.[56]

The Happiness Frenzy

Regardless of how one felt about happiness, there was sufficient evidence to believe that Americans' interest in the emotion was at an all-time high as the Obamas moved into the White House. Some were arguing that our pursuit of happiness had gone too far, while others were saying that having yet more of it would be a good thing for individuals and society; such conflicting views suggested that, no matter one's opinion, the subject was a passionate one. Although research had over the years made it consistently clear that demographics of any type made little difference in determining one's level of happiness, much was being made of a new study indicating that American women now had less of it than their male counterparts. In their "The Paradox of Declining Female Happiness," Betsey Stevenson and Justin Wolfers of The Wharton School argued that women were less happy than they used to be and were likely to be even less happy as they aged. Notable journalists Maureen Dowd and Arianna Huffington believed the findings of the study had merit (the latter writing that the research revealed "the sad, shocking truth about how women are feeling"), further stirring up the pot of happiness as related to gender.[57]

Adding some much needed common sense to the situation, Katha Pollitt steered the conversation to the broader issue of happiness research in general. "What a stupid question," she hypothetically answered the question, "Are you happy?" thinking there were a host of problems when it came to researchers' attempts to measure an individual's level of happiness. The first and biggest problem was, of course, how one defined the term, tossing up "content," "joyful," "hopeful," and "relieved" as just a few perfectly valid but wildly different ways to describe happiness. When she was asked, and even who was asking the question, were other methodological considerations that went into answering the question, she pointed out in *The Nation* in 2009, thinking studies like "The Paradox of Declining Female Happiness" should not be taken too seriously (or taken at all) because of the major challenges facing all researchers in the field. Pollitt felt she could have "a dozen different answers to the question, 'Are you happy?'" that exposed the bad research practices that had been relied upon in the field since the first studies were done in the 1920s.[58]

Indeed, often left out of studies of and conversations about happiness was its most important characteristic: its subjective nature. One person's brand of happiness could be entirely different than that of another person, a fact that was typically ignored by researchers and critics alike when they proposed their weighty thoughts on the matter. The more fundamental problem with making conclusions about happiness was that people often did not tell the truth to researchers about any topic, especially one as sensitive as whether one was a happy person or not. Longitudinal comparisons of happiness were especially silly, as there were an infinite array of variables that went into the reporting and measurement of an individual's emotion at any given time in any given place. Beyond constantly shifting social, economic, political, scientific, technological, and cultural winds, the very concept of happiness could (and did) change over time, making any sweeping generalizations about the subject highly suspect.[59]

The inherent problems associated with discussing and debating happiness were immaterial to those determined to capitalize on the popularity of the subject. "Welcome to the happiness frenzy," Carlin Flora wrote for *Psychology Today* in 2009, thinking that despite their best efforts to get happier over the past decade, Americans had "remarkably little to show for it." Flora reported that some four thousand books about happiness had been published in 2008 while just fifty had been in 2000, this eighty-fold increase an obvious sign of consumers' greater interest in the subject within a relatively short stretch of time. While it was difficult to believe these numbers, it did indeed appear that happiness in America was in a kind of frenzied state. Besides the flurry in publishing, courses in positive psychology at the country's colleges and universities, and the life coach trend, many Americans were attending happiness workshops in hopes to learn how they could acquire greater quantities of the emotion. Was there any limit in terms of how much happiness help Americans could consume?[60]

If past was prologue, the answer to that question would definitely be no. "A shallow sea of yellow smiley faces, self-help gurus, and purveyors of kitchen-table wisdom have strip-mined the science, extracted a lot of fool's gold, and stormed the marketplace with guarantees to annihilate your worry, stress, anguish, dejection, and even ennui," she wrote, seeing no end in sight to the feeding frenzy of happiness. Despite all the money and effort that had been directed to this aggressive pursuit of happiness, some evidence suggested that Americans as a group had not only not progressed but perhaps even regressed. Americans' inclination to nip any kind of negative feeling in the bud clearly wasn't working, reason enough to believe those making the case that inhabiting the darker side of our emotional radius was a natural and perhaps necessary part of the human experience.[61]

Nobody arguably more than Barbara Ehrenreich subscribed to the idea that a little (or a lot of) grouchiness and grumpiness went a long way. In her latest book, *Bright-Sided: How Relentless Promotion of Positive Thinking Has Undermined America*, the author and activist attacked all the positivity that was being pushed by the happiness set, arguing that it was having the opposite effect of what was intended. Positive psychology and the other branches growing off the tree of happiness represented a form of dumbing down that was bad for America and Americans, Ehrenreich believed, calling our obsession with the sunny side of life a "mass delusion." Serious problems were going unaddressed because of this blind optimism, she maintained, seeing a real cost to the country's relentless pursuit of happiness.[62]

Ehrenreich would no doubt have become even surlier to read Walter Mosley's piece titled "Get Happy" in *The Nation*. "Americans deserve a government agency charged with fostering the pursuit of happiness," Mosley declared, thinking that it was time to assign a federal department to help turn Jefferson's rhetoric into reality. One might have thought that Mosley, who served on that publication's editorial board when he was not writing bestselling mysteries and detective novels, was joking, but he was clearly not. The Declaration of Independence stated that the pursuit of happiness was an "inalienable right," making it for Mosley "a government responsibility to ensure that all Americans, or as many as possible, are given a clear path toward that pursuit." Americans were "an unhappy, unhealthy lot," he believed, good reason for a new branch of government to be created that would work in concert with our executive, legislative, and judicial branches. "If we can, through a central agency, begin to come to a general awareness of what we need to clear the path to the pursuit of happiness," Mosley wrote, "I believe that the lives we are living stand a chance of being more satisfying."[63]

While Mosley's proposal was rather remarkable given the growing sentiment that there was already too much pressure being placed on Americans to be happy, this was not the first time a proposal was made for a government to get into the happiness business. In 1972, King Wangchuck of Bhutan determined that rather than attempt to maximize its gross national product, the small nation in the Himalayas would prioritize "gross national happiness" in its official policy making. Guided by a philosophy of Buddhist enlightenment versus economic progress, measures to preserve the environment, regulate tourism, and fund health care and education were put in place to strive for high levels of "GNH" versus "GNP." Cultural traditions and national pride were at least as important as the amount of currency in the country's coffers, the king and Bhutan's subsequent leaders believed, thinking that GNH was more likely than GNP to make its citizens happy people.[64]

Bhutan was one thing, of course, but would such a Zen philosophy work in a much larger Western country? Richard Layard, a prominent British economist and author of the 2005 *Happiness: Lessons from a New Science*, certainly thought so. "Happiness should become the goal of policy," he wrote in the book, "and the progress of national happiness should be measured and analysed as closely as the growth of GNP."[65] Even Ed Diener was making a case for a "national index of happiness" that would offer a government a means of evaluating policies based on how they furthered citizens' sense of well-being.[66] Until such a radical idea was put in place, however, it was up to individual Americans to try to find their own happiness, something they continued to do with gusto in the decade that lay ahead.

HAPPILY EVER AFTER, 2010–

Perhaps it is the greatest marketing slogan of all time. —Lauren Sandler, referring to "the pursuit of happiness," in 2011

I n 2010, much was made in publishing circles when an international bestseller titled *Hector and the Search for Happiness* finally hit American bookstores. In the book, which was compared to *The Little Prince* because of its peripatetic charm, Hector, a discontented psychiatrist, goes to the four corners of the Earth in search of happiness. Best of all, Hector keeps a journal of what he has learned, with the most valuable lessons passed on to readers by author (and real-life French psychiatrist) François Lelord. "It's a mistake to think that happiness is the goal," goes Lesson #7, with Hector acquiring the knowledge that becoming a happy person is more a by-product of a life well lived versus an endpoint. Lesson #10 is the equally wise, "Happiness is doing a job you love," in which Hector observes that the happiest people tend be those who are engrossed in whatever professional path they have chosen. In Lesson #13, readers learn that "happiness is feeling useful to others," a result of Hector noticing that the subjective state of being was most likely to be realized by those who are not focused on themselves.[1]

Hector may have learned how to be happy on his fictional search around the world, but real-life Americans have not enjoyed nearly as much success. Happiness has continued to take new twists and turns on its rollercoaster ride this past decade, evolving into a full-fledged global movement with its own set of controversial politics. Happiness has become increasingly institutionalized, it's fair to say, as governments and universities attempt to take ownership of what had been primarily an individual pursuit. Growing numbers of positive psychologists too have put claims on happiness, infusing it with Buddhism-inspired mindfulness and other techniques designed to help those who want to live happier lives. The ascent of information technology in recent years, especially the wild popularity of the smartphone and social media, has also redirected the cultural trajectory of happiness. Despite all this, happiness in America has moved backward rather than forward in the early twenty-first century, signs that we the people may never achieve the degree of it that we feel entitled to. Will Americans ever live happily ever after?

The Politics of Happiness

While Americans seeking greater happiness could certainly have picked up a few useful pointers from Hector's journey, others might have consulted Carol Graham's *Happiness Around the World*. Graham explored in depth "the paradox of happy peasants and miserable millionaires," as the book's subtitle read, probing the reasons why a good many poor people on the planet were seemingly happier than rich people. "Higher per capita income levels do not translate directly into higher average happiness levels," Graham plainly put it after comparing levels of each between Nigerians and Japanese, Bangladeshis and Russians, Panamanians and Argentines, and many other nationalities. Genetics and adaption each played larger roles in determining an individual's level of happiness than money, she concluded, more evidence that Americans' general belief that having more of the latter would make them happier was a false assumption.[2]

In his *The Politics of Happiness: What Government Can Learn from the New Research on Well-Being*, Derek Bok also investigated why Americans, given their collective wealth, were far from being the happiest people on Earth. Revisiting the research showing that greater prosperity had not made Americans any happier since the 1950s, Bok, ex-president of Harvard, questioned the very motives of our capitalist system. If "rising incomes have failed to make Americans happier over the last fifty years," he reasonably asked, "what is the point of working such long hours and risking environmental disaster in order to keep on doubling and redoubling our Gross Domestic Product?" Perhaps economic growth should not be the primary objective of governmental policy, Bok proposed, a radical notion that was likely inspired by Bhutan's decision to prioritize gross national happiness over gross national product in order to better serve its citizens.[3]

New research related to personal and national happiness made it abundantly clear that one didn't have to be a socialist to have reservations about the fundamentals of consumer capitalism. Writing for *Forbes* that same year, Harvard Business School professor Michael I. Norton argued that money could buy happiness but only if it was spent on others. Once someone hit the median income level (around $60,000 in the United States at the time), there were only negligible increases in happiness as income rose, his research showed, with having more money simply leading to having more stuff. Spending money on others typically led to much greater levels of happiness regardless of how much was spent, however, lending more support to the idea that those looking to the marketplace to become happier were looking in the wrong place, unless they were shopping for someone else.[4] A new study completed by economist Angus Deaton and Daniel Kahneman reported similar findings, although the two Princeton professors capped the "income of happiness" level at $75,000 per household.[5]

If money didn't buy happiness, as so many were saying, why then were a good number of Americans intent on acquiring as much as possible? Roya Wolverson of *Time* believed it had much to do with "scorekeeping" (i.e., that the keep-up-with-the-Joneses ethos was still very much alive in the country). Popular culture, specifically reality TV, reinforced and intensified this drive to move up the economic ladder, preferably with haste, she felt, the result an overemphasis on the making and spending of money. The notion that Americans just didn't know what would make them happy was another factor in the struggle to find happiness. "We are doing things with our money that make us happy in the moment, but that's not always the best strategy for long-term well-being," Michael Norton told Wolverson, too many of us interested in simply satisfying a craving rather than investing in things that would offer lasting fulfillment.[6]

While the relationship between happiness and money continued to be explored, much in part because it appeared that the relationship was less intimate than we believed or liked to believe, others were more interested in the former's philosophical underpinnings. In her book *Exploring Happiness: From Aristotle to Brain Science*, Sissela Bok made a convincing case that we were living in a golden age of happiness. "Not since antiquity have there been such passionate debates as those taking place today about contending visions of what makes for human happiness," the senior visiting fellow at Harvard (and wife of Derek Bok) wrote, comparing more informed twenty-first-century students of the subject to the likes of Confucius, Buddha, Lao-Tzu, and Socrates. Bok traced the arc of happiness from the sixth century BC to contemporary times, arguing that an individual's conception and definition of happiness revealed much about the identity of that person.[7]

While dinner table conversation in the Bok household was no doubt fascinating as the two scholars wrote their respective books about happiness, other modern-day thinkers contributed their thoughts on the subject. Americans had a special relationship with happiness, everyone would agree, making a deeper understanding of how the emotion was expressed in this country an excellent way to add to the field's body of knowledge. Like the American Dream, Lauren Sandler proposed in *Psychology Today* in 2011, "the pursuit of happiness" had become charged with a strong sense of expectations, with many Americans feeling they were entitled to realize their particular version of "the good life." But while happiness had risen in much of the world in recent decades, Americans had stalled or even gone backward on that dimension, cause to take a long, hard look at our way of life. The pressures of family life and work were (and remain) great, making it no wonder that many Americans were (and are) falling short in their personal pursuit of happiness.[8]

Perhaps after reading Derek Bok's *The Politics of Happiness* and finding it to be more than just interesting intellectual fodder, none other than President Barack Obama decided to step into the happiness breach by exploring potential ways the book's conclusions could shape public policy. In 2012, the Obama administration's Department of Health and Human Services gathered a group of "experts" to "define reliable measures of 'subjective well-being,'" the goal being to compile "official statistics" regarding Americans' happiness or lack thereof. Further down the road, presumably, the federal government could create economic and social policies designed to make Americans happier, again maybe taking a cue of how leaders of tiny Bhutan were approaching what was in the best interests of its people. David Cameron, the conservative prime minister of the United Kingdom, was pursuing a similar path by urging his government to evaluate the happiness of British citizens for the same ends, as were policymakers in France and Canada.[9]

Not surprisingly, American conservatives had a field day with this piece of news first reported in the *Washington Post*. "Happiness? What business is that of the government?" asked Wesley J. Smith in *The Weekly Standard* in 2012, thinking that "defining measures of subjective well-being is only the first step." Much like how columnist Russell Baker mocked LBJ's 1965 announced plan to study Americans' happiness with potential applications for his "Great Society" program, Smith semi-joked that the new title of Alan Krueger, the president's chief economic adviser, would be "Happiness Czar." "Once the government decides what makes us happy and begins to collect data and publish statistics about how we are doing happiness-wise as a society," he fretted, "the inevitable next step will be to uncover a crisis, which new policies and bureaucracies will be required to cure." Messing with Americans' happiness smacked of technocracy and demagoguery, the senior fellow at the Discovery Institute's Center on Human Exceptionalism believed, seeing any attempt to regulate the emotion as a very bad idea.[10]

Happiness Quantified

Smith was likely not pleased to hear that a few American cities were already moving ahead with making happiness their business. In 2011, for example, Eau Claire, Wisconsin, had formed what it called a "happiness partnership" involving the city's government, the University of Wisconsin, the public library, the chamber of commerce, and a disparate group of other organizations. City officials first surveyed residents on a number of dimensions related to well-being, with the results discussed in town forums in order to decide what next steps should be taken. Community and public life were at the heart of Eau Claire's effort to make the happiness of its citizens a priority, with cultural events, festivals, and the arts deemed a good way to achieve that. City officials in Nevada City, California, meanwhile, polled its residents to learn what made them happy, using the findings from the survey to determine if and how further development should proceed. And in Seattle, something called the Happiness Initiative was making some headway, with the results of its survey of citizens to be used by local council members in creating public policy. Progressives were pleased as punch to hear of such initiatives, thinking they served as indications that Americans were ready for a brand of politics grounded in the enabling of happiness. Happiness was well on the way to becoming a form of activism, one could say, with left-leaners urging all Americans to celebrate "Pursuit of Happiness Day" on April 13 (Jefferson's birthday).[11]

While liberals and conservatives debated the merits of such a new and perhaps radical kind of politics, psychologists and economists continued to make inroads into what they seriously considered to be a genuine, albeit new science. Unfortunately, however, research methods in happiness had in many cases not advanced much since academics wandered into the field in the 1920s. Ranking oneself as "not too happy," "pretty happy," or "very happy" was primitive at best, with good reason to be suspect and skeptical of any and all findings gleaned. Quantifying an individual's level of happiness was, as Katha Pollitt had pointed out, a silly exercise that reduced a person's unique personality and situation in life to a meaningless number. That did not stop many researchers from using such a 1-2-3 scale and give it the scientific-sounding name of "hedonics," perhaps in hopes that doing so would lead to tenure and keep the grant money flowing (there was actually a textbook on the subject: Bernard van Praag's and Ada Ferrer-i-Carbonell's *Happiness Quantified: A Satisfaction Calculus Approach*). "The brisk adding up by utilitarians of sexual pleasure and career satisfaction and family love and the exercise of vital powers . . . does not make a lot of sense," Deirdre N. McCloskey observed in *The New Republic* in 2012, thinking the recent wave of supposedly empirical "happyism" to be not just methodologically challenged but downright "creepy."[12]

Perhaps the biggest problem of trying to quantify happiness was that most Americans didn't themselves know if they were happy or not. It was not unusual for people to frequently wonder "Am I happy?"

not an easy question to answer given the constantly shifting variables of money, health, work, romance, family, friends, or just the relative horribleness of that morning's commute. In his 2012 *Satisfaction* Not *Guaranteed*, social historian Peter N. Stearns made the interesting case that Americans' increasingly desperate pursuit of happiness has come at the same time as the opportunities to catch it have grown. While the desperation could be seen in actual book titles such as *Baby Steps to Happiness, Infinite Happiness, Absolute Happiness, Happiness Is Your Destiny*, and *Happiness Is a Serious Problem*, contemporary Americans have decades longer to realize happiness than those a century earlier simply by the nature of greater longevity. Any way one measured it— wealth, health, material abundance, gender and race equality, or simply the ability to get a good cup of coffee at any one of the more than eleven thousand Starbucks in the country—the chances to be happy for the average American were, at least on paper, better than ever.[13]

From some of the personal stories being told, those using the increasingly popular technique of mindful meditation were realizing considerable success in finding greater happiness in their lives. The Buddhist practice was based on devoting one's fullest attention to the present moment, with enthusiasts finding that forgetting the past and not worrying about the future reduced stress and chased away "negative" emotions like anger and envy. Neuroscience was proving that mindful meditation had all kinds of health benefits, including boosting one's immune system and slowing down one's pulse, and was even capable of physically reshaping the brain for the better. Buddhist monks had known about the positive effects of meditating upon mind, body, and soul for centuries, but now ordinary Americans, including many children, were embracing what was often simply called "mindfulness."[14]

With no magic happiness pill yet to be invented, practicing techniques like mindful meditation was considered by a growing number of Americans to be well worth the time and effort. That part of the brain responsible for pleasure and the biochemistry associated with it had been discovered decades back, but the much-anticipated neurological revolution in happiness had not taken place. Scientists had learned how to elevate feelings of pleasure by stimulating certain areas of the brain, but the effects wore off as soon as those procedures were stopped. Tinkering with the mechanics of the brain was a much more difficult undertaking than originally believed, they gradually learned, and human happiness appeared to consist of more than some electrical prodding of the nucleus accumbens and cingulate cortex. "Although scientists have made some progress in uncovering the biological basis of hedonia [pleasure], we know very little about how the brain gives rise to a broader sense of a life well lived," Morten L. Kringelbach and Kent C. Berridge wrote in *Scientific American* in 2012, hopeful that the secrets to happiness would one day be uncovered.[15]

The Happiness of Pursuit

Until then, experts armed with the latest research offered additional advice on how Americans might go about their personal pursuit of happiness. Todd Kashdan, the George Mason psychology professor, was now suggesting that for some it might be best to go after a different, more reachable goal. "Trying to make happiness your objective in life is problematic," he told *Psychology Today* in 2013, proposing "curiosity" or "sense of purpose" as possible alternatives. For many, happiness was just too variable an emotion to be continually maintained, Kashdan believed, with everything from a bad night's sleep to a cloudy day able to throw one off course. Happiness was so central to American identity that it was highly unusual to challenge the idea that each and every citizen should make it his or her grand mission, making Kashdan's take on the matter a welcome surprise.[16]

Sonja Lyubomirsky also advised Americans to curb their enthusiasm when it came to happiness. Continually questioning whether one was happy or not was not a good way to go about realizing more of it, the University of California–Riverside psychology professor opined, with too many of us obsessing where we were on the happiness scale at any given moment. Stick to the basics—being kind, forming and deepening relationships, and enjoying the simple things—she recommended, with happiness more likely to come incidentally than as a purposeful goal. Contradictorily, however, Yuna Ferguson, another authority on the subject, argued that consciously striving for happiness was the better path to take. Choosing to be happier could "serve as the impetus for cognitive and behavioral changes that eventually facilitate greater well-being," she observed in an essay titled "Trying to Be Happier Really Can Work" published in *The Journal of Positive Psychology*, supporting proactive techniques like mindfulness.[17]

Framing happiness as something that could be achieved with dedicated effort meshed nicely with Americans' can-do spirit, far better in fact than what might be called the "happiness-is-a-by-product" school of thought. "Knowing what gives your life meaning and what gives you a sense of purpose is the path to finding your happiness," Susan Graves stated in *Prevention*, telling those readers desiring greater happiness that they better go after it if they intended to land it. The to-do lists we carried in our brains everyday were good for getting things done but left us directionless, she believed, basing her view on a study done at the University of Wisconsin. Researchers there found that people with a strong sense of purpose in life were also most likely to be happy, with other research suggesting that those who had a good reason to get out of bed in the morning tended to live longer.[18]

The different and sometimes conflicting views on how to best attain more happiness in one's life were indications that the subject remained of great interest to many Americans. The sheer volume of material related to happiness was still growing, in fact, with seemingly no amount of information that could possibly be of value to readers, viewers, and users able to meet the demand. *Time* had devoted a special issue to happiness in 2005, but eight years later editors of the magazine decided so much had happened in the field since then that it was time for another. Cleverly calling the issue "The Happiness of Pursuit," *Time* offered readers an overview of the current science of the field as well as how social upheaval interacted with personal happiness. As always, the relationship between happiness and money was plumbed, but it was another dynamic—the relationship between happiness and social media—that was perhaps most interesting and relevant to everyday life.[19]

By twisting Jefferson's phrase around, the magazine's editors made it clear that happiness was more about its pursuit than its realization. Americans were spending billions of dollars a year trying to get happier, but had precious little to show for it. The United States currently ranked twenty-third in global happiness, according to the World Happiness Report (which was published by the Sustainable Development Solutions Network and endorsed by the United Nations), reason to wonder if one might be better off relocating to a happier place like Malaysia, Tanzania, or Vietnam. Did Americans' heavy use of social media have something to do with the downward trajectory of happiness in the country on a comparative basis? Sixty-two percent of Americans had a social media presence in 2013, after all, a significantly higher number than in many countries in the report.[20] Perhaps that was so, given that social media could very well make one think or feel that other people had more and better stuff, were more popular, and, maybe worst of all, were having way more fun in life. With over a billion people on Facebook alone, it was easy to conclude that one was not one of the happiest (or even happier) persons on Earth. The numbers seemed to bear this out: in a poll conducted for the magazine, 60 percent of those surveyed reported that they did not feel better about themselves after spending time on social media.[21]

It was surprising that, given the steps many Americans were taking, happiness in the nation appeared to be heading south rather than north (optimism, for example, which many experts correlated with happiness, had dropped significantly over the past decade, according to *Time*'s poll). To boost their level of happiness, Americans were looking to pharmaceuticals (one-fourth of the women in the country were on antidepressants), food (almost half the population ate to improve their mood), and self-improvement (now estimated to be a $10 billion-a-year industry). "The pursuit of happiness, once an ideal, has become a big business but not an especially effective one," the magazine noted, suggesting the gap between overly optimistic expectations and reality was making many marketers wealthy but not making many Americans any happier.[22]

Because some degree of happiness could be obtained from a wide variety of sources, quantifying the size of the industry dedicated to it was difficult. A sampling of the latest happiness how-tos revealed that while some of the sizzle had changed, the steak was much the same as it was in ancient times when philosophers like Euripides doled out wisdom on the subject. BookScan, which tracked industry sales, did not have data specifically on books about happiness, but self-help overall was up 12 percent in 2014 versus the previous year, quite a jump. "Has the happiness market reached the saturation point?" asked Andrea Sachs in *Publishers Weekly* that year, wondering how many more books on the subject Americans could read. One publisher believed many more, citing ever-increasing email and social media as forces driving growth in the segment.[23]

While motivational cheerleading remained a large part of happiness publishing, the advancement of neuroscience was also being credited for the greater number of books about happiness being written and read. Brain research added empirical evidence to what had been mostly fluffy, inspirational material, taking the genre to another level. In her *The Sweet Spot*, for example, sociologist Christine Carter deftly translated relevant findings from neuroscience into practical terms, showing readers how it was in the best interest of their respective brains to lower their "busyness" quotient. In *Four Ways to Click*, meanwhile, neurobiologist Amy Banks drew on her background as an instructor in psychiatry at Harvard Medical School to show that happy brains tended to be relationship-oriented.[24] There was hard science behind the previously "soft" emotion of happiness, many authors with advanced degrees were saying, more reason why readers were taking their prescriptions to heart.

A Grey Mushy Process

Scientifically grounded or not, more critics were resenting and resisting the unrelenting pressure for everyone to be happy. "Nothing depresses me more than reading about happiness," Alison Beard observed in the *Harvard Business Review* in 2015, the backlash against "feel goodism" very much in play. Almost fifteen thousand books were then listed in the "happiness" subgenre of self-help books on Amazon (there are now over twenty thousand), and fifty-five TED talks on the subject available for viewing on its website (now hundreds). The problem for Beard was that there were too many correct answers (health, money, social connection, purpose, "flow," generosity, gratitude, inner peace, and positive thinking, to name just some) to the question "What makes us happy?" "Social scientists tell us that even the simplest tricks—counting our blessings, meditating for 10 minutes a day, forcing smiles—can push us into a happier state of mind," she wrote, wondering why despite all this advice most Americans (including herself) still found happiness to be difficult or impossible to find. On the surface, Beard, like many of us, believed she had all the ingredients to be happy, but turning them into a reliable recipe for happiness was simpler said than done even with the new and improved how-tos being published.[25]

In fact, Beard, senior editor at the *HBR*, felt that what she called "the huge and growing body of happiness literature" was making things worse rather than better. Telling people that they should be happy when they already knew that was just rubbing their lack of happiness in, she maintained, all this supposed self-help having exactly the opposite effect than intended. Beard was just one of a growing number of critics claiming their right not to be totally happy all the time. The backlash against prescribed happiness that had begun in 2008 had by 2015 become a cottage industry unto itself as more people who valued "negativity" made their voices heard. New books such as Gabriele Oettingen's *Rethinking Positive Thinking*, Todd Kashdan's and Robert Biswas-Diener's *The Upside of Your Dark Side*, Kelly McGonigal's *The Upside of Stress*, Anthony Seldon's *Beyond Happiness*, and, last but not least, William Davies's *The Happiness Industry* all denounced the public mandate to strive for greater happiness and positivism at the cost of other pursuits.[26]

While sharing the central theme of pushing back against the mass marketing of happiness, each of these books approached it in a different way. Oettingen, a psychology professor at NYU, argued that regular reality checks served as a better way of reaching one's goals than living in a dreamland of constructed happiness, while Kashdan and Biswas-Diener demonstrated that supposed negative emotions actually served valuable psychic ends. McGonigal, meanwhile, focused on stress, specifically how it could be converted into something that was beneficial rather than harmful to our mental and physical health. Selden advised readers to move beyond the quest for pleasure and instead go after deeper emotional experiences, while Davies attacked what he saw as the corporatization of happiness. Together these books represented an important body of work that challenged the turning of what Davies called "a grey mushy process inside our brains" into a goal that many Americans believed they had an obligation to try to reach.[27]

With book titles like *How to Be Happy, Dammit* (seriously), one didn't have to be an expert to conclude that at some point Americans' pursuit became an obsession. Besides the general feeling of some critics that there was much more to life than chasing happiness, there was growing evidence that much of the $10 billion Americans were spending on self-help as a whole was a waste of good money. "New research suggests that the more you go looking for happiness, the less likely you are to find it," reported Mandy Oaklander in *Time* in 2015 after reading an article published in the *Journal of Experimental Psychology*. Among Americans, "desperately wanting to be happy is linked with lower psychological health," Brett Ford, the author of the study, wrote, the kicker being that precisely the opposite held true for Russians and East Asians. While happiness was a social construct in the East, it was typically an individual one in the West, Ford explained, making Americans far more likely to be disappointed when everything didn't go their way.[28]

While some experts in happiness clung to the idea that, as with other goals, one better have a solid plan and be highly motivated if one was to reach it, most in the field were now concluding that directly pursuing a subjective state of well-being was an ill-advised strategy. Jennifer Moss, cofounder and COO of Plasticity Labs ("a technology startup on a mission to give 1 billion people the tools to live a happier, higher-performing life"), compared happiness to a fog that dissipates the closer one got to it. Trying to grab onto happiness would only leave one with a handful of air, she posited in the *Harvard Business Review*, reason that we needed to rethink the very concept of the emotion. Rather than embrace the cheery, smiley-face notion of happiness, Moss suggested, we should relocate the emotion along a spectrum of "good" and "bad" feelings and experiences. There was indeed research showing that positive mental and physical well-being was correlated with a philosophy of "taking the good with the bad," supporting the growing sentiment that Americans' interpretation of happiness was far too unidimensional.[29]

Shawn Achor, a researcher and corporate trainer, agreed that chasing happiness was missing the larger point. "The biggest misconception of the happiness industry is that happiness is an end, not a means," he stated, with most Americans instructed to believe that they would be happy if they got what they wanted. The brain just didn't work that way, however, a prime example of the neuroscience showing that our minds operated in a much more illogical, emotion-driven fashion than we liked to think. In linguistic terms, it was better to approach the subject more as a verb than as a noun (i.e., to do those things that made us happy rather than attempt to realize a state of happiness). "We're happiest when we're not thinking about it, when we're enjoying the present moment because we're lost in a meaningful project, working toward a higher goal, or helping someone who needs us," Moss concluded after talking with Achor and other experts, words that Americans were increasingly hearing but for the most part not heeding.[30]

Interestingly, while Americans wanted to find happiness, they seemed to want no such thing for fictional characters. "Happy endings" were decidedly out in romance novels and had been for some time, one author of that genre noted, wondering why the publishing community was so anti-happiness. "When did happiness fall out of fashion?" Marie Bostwick asked readers of *Publishers Weekly*, puzzled why it was disdained in contemporary literature yet so highly desired in real life. Readers in the nineteenth century expected things to work out well for protagonists in novels, something not-too-shabby authors like Charles Dickens and Jane Austen knew quite well. At some point, however, "tying things up with a big bow," as one critic put it, became seen as a pretentious conceit and a sign of bad writing. Bostwick defended the happy ending, thinking it was not just a perfectly legitimate literary technique but also served a valuable social purpose by, in her own words, "providing hope [and] instilling the belief that obstacles can be overcome, love can last, fences can be mended, and good can triumph." "If there is no possibility of a happy ending," she concluded, "what is the point of striving for one?"[31]

A GPS for Your Soul

Bostwick could have taken comfort in the fact that real-life Americans were not at all ready to give up striving for happiness. While novels may not have been a good source to find it, many Americans were now looking to technology for help in their pursuit. With mobile devices now in most people's hands for many hours during a day, it was inevitable that apps promising users enhanced happiness would be brought to the marketplace. "Your next mood boost could be right in the palm of your hand, thanks to a slew of new apps designed to bring you joy," gushed *Health* in 2017, advising readers to check out iTunes and Google Play to find "apps that make you happy." "Happier," for example, regularly reminded users to "notice the sunny moments in every day" and then file them in a built-in gratitude journal, while "The Happiness Planner" offered users an opportunity to "put joy on your schedule" via a calendar, to-do list, and daily reflections.[32] *Health* magazine had in fact glommed onto happiness in a big way by devoting much of its content to the subject and even making "Happy Begins Here" its slogan. "Happiness is the foundation of wellness," Clare McHugh explained to readers, seeing the magazine she edited as "a GPS for your soul."[33]

It could be understood how, given Americans' widespread yearning for happiness and fondness for mobile devices, such apps seemed like a great idea. In 2017, a company called Happy Money introduced an app called "Joy," which was intended to help users spend and save their money based on their respective personality profiles. "'Joy' is the first app that doesn't judge you, but instead embraces you for who you are and what makes YOU [his emphasis] happy," exclaimed Scott Saunders, founder and CEO of Happy Money, noting that the iOS application was the brainchild of his company's team of clinical psychologists and neuroscientists. "It's not about how much money is in your account, it's about how much happiness there is in your life," added professor Elizabeth Dunn, PhD, Joy's scientific advisor and author of *Happy Money: The Science of Happier Spending.*[34]

Happiness apps were all fine and good for those seeking greater serenity but they paled in comparison to the "100 Days of Happiness" social media craze that took off sometime during the summer of 2016. Those wanting to embark on the challenge to be happy for one hundred consecutive days typed in the hashtag "100 happy days" on their various devices, with participants then posting on social media what had made them happy that day. Young people especially were attracted to the phenomenon that had clear links to the positive psychology movement so popular on college campuses, with many finding the experience to be truly revelatory.[35]

While millennials posted their daily missives of happiness, Donna Freitas convincingly argued that such use of social media carried a darker side. "Because young people feel so pressured to post happy things on social media, most of what everyone sees on social media from their peers are happy things," Freitas wrote in her *The Happiness Effect* after extensive research with college students, the result being that "they often feel inferior because they aren't actually happy all the time." Everyone knew that identities presented on Facebook, Instagram, and other social media were typically not representative of real selves but rather carefully edited, happycentric versions of people's lives. Freitas suggested that social media actually lowered the degree of happiness of users rather than raised it, and advised young people to unplug as much as possible.[36]

On the heels of *The Happiness Effect* came Jean M. Twenge's *iGen*, another book arguing that technology had made young people less happy. Not just the time spent on social media but on smartphones in general was making millennials lonelier and more stressed, her research showed.

There was a dramatic shift in behavior in 2011–2012 when smartphones became ubiquitous, the psychologist suggested, and not for the better. "Teens who spend more time on screen activities are more likely to be unhappy, and those who spend more time on nonscreen activities are more likely to be more happy," Twenge plainly put it, concluding that greater connectivity was ironically fueling greater isolation.[37]

It is likely no coincidence that the failure of students' various devices to make them any happier has led to significantly greater opportunities for them to learn how to be happy in a formal setting. Happiness has continued to infiltrate the nation's education system, even becoming part of the curricula at some of the country's elite medical schools. At Stanford's School of Medicine, for example, Thupten Jinpa, a former Buddhist monk with a PhD in religious studies from Cambridge University, is teaching future physicians the art of compassion for both their own good and that of their patients. "It's the key to happiness and well-being," Jinpa explained, with much research showing that feeling empathy for another person's misfortune offered a host of physical and mental health benefits.[38] At Harvard, meanwhile, plans were announced in 2016 to create a center to study happiness and health with the purpose of learning how related they were. Backed by a $21 million donation, Harvard was hiring researchers from many fields including psychology, medicine, and sociology for its new Lee Kum Sheung Center for Health and Happiness that would be part of the university's school of public health.[39]

Happiness is gradually becoming more accepted as a legitimate academic field much in part due to remarkable students like Kiera Peltz. As a high school student in California, Peltz worked for a local congressman, sparking her interest in how government could best improve the lives of citizens. Her next move was to Brown University, where, after deciding that political science was too narrow of a major, she created an independent concentration in happiness. Focusing on why government did not appear to make citizens any happier, Peltz wrote her thesis on ways lawmakers could utilize happiness research to inform their policy making process. "Obviously now, more than ever, (considering) how divisive American politics is, happiness is needed," Peltz remarked, her long-term plan to go into politics after getting her PhD.[40]

No doubt noticing how students were lining up for Tal Ben-Shahar's class in happiness at Harvard, administrators at Yale University decided to offer a similar course grounded in the tenets of positive psychology. In January 2018, twelve hundred students—one-fourth of that university's undergraduates—enrolled in "Psychology and the Good Life," taught by psychology professor Laurie Santos. Twice a week, the students heard Santos lecture on how to be a happier person, a desire so great that the class turned out to be the most popular in Yale's three-hundred-plus-year history. "Our intuitions about what will make us happy, like winning the lottery and getting a good grade, are totally wrong," Santos told the *New York Times*, hoping that Yale's high achievers would reject other-directed narratives of happiness and discover their own, personally defined versions.[41]

The Overarching Motivator

Alongside the remarkable ascent and popularity of happiness studies has come the full embrace of the emotion within the nation's business community. As the United Nations' 2013 declaration of March 20 as the International Day of Happiness (or just Happiness Day) gained traction, marketers looked for opportunities to tie into the event. In March 2016, for example, fifty-six billboards were put up in forty-one cities across the United States as part of the celebration of the day set aside to "recognize the relevance of happiness and well-being as universal human goals." The billboards were intended to spread "joy, optimism, and inspiration" and help Americans "celebrate and rekindle their inner joy," as the public relations release for the promotion explained, but there appeared to be a secondary agenda. The cosponsors of the billboards were The Joy Team—a "positive thought nonprofit" based in Vancouver, Washington—and Natural Life—a retailer of artisan "happy treasures" based in Ponte Vedra Beach, Florida. "One positive message can make a huge difference in someone's day," said Michele McKeag Larsen, founder of The Joy Team, with the signs expected to generate about seventeen million impressions over the course of the four-week campaign.[42]

Other marketers looked to the International Day of Happiness as an ideal vehicle by which to promote their products. The day had the blessing of the United Nations, after all, giving it an aura of world peace and global harmony, the stuff of many marketers' dreams. On Happiness Day 2017, ProFlowers, part of FTD, the floral and gifting company, handed out roses to ten thousand rather taken aback New Yorkers, a random act of kindness that hustling and bustling Gothamites were not at all used to. "At ProFlowers, we're in the flower gifting business—but more importantly, we're in the business of making people happy," said the company's general manager, Senior Vice President Laura Szeliga, citing research indicating that not just receiving but giving flowers made people happy.[43] Driscolls, a top seller of berries, meanwhile, was doing its own research and finding that its product was also linked to happiness. Eighty-five percent of Americans surveyed agreed that "eating berries makes them happy," the company announced in 2106, going as far as to claim that there was a "direct connection between eating berries and joy."[44]

While such one-offs were certainly opportunistic, no media company had yet to try to "own" happiness until the arrival of *Live Happy* magazine in 2013. Since premiering in October of that year, *Live Happy* has served as arguably the loudest voice of the happiness movement (the magazine is owned by Live Happy LLC, a Dallas-based company dedicated to "promoting and sharing authentic happiness through education, integrity, gratitude and community awareness" by "bringing the happiness movement to a personal level and inspiring people to engage in purpose-driven, healthy, meaningful lives"). Each and every issue, the bimonthly features people who are "living happy," inspiration for readers wishing they could find such lasting happiness. As well, expert advice drawn from the science of happiness can be regularly found in the magazine's paper or digital pages, this too designed to help readers become happier people. There is also a Live Happy weekly podcast, book, and website, making the brand an emerging empire of happiness.[45] Every March, to celebrate the International Day of Happiness, Live Happy pulls out all the stops with its #HappyActs campaign. While the company posts "happy learnings" on social media and the magazine's website, people everywhere have the opportunity to put up their own simple ways to happiness on more than a hundred "happiness walls" scattered across the globe.[46] With Live Happy, it can be said that happiness is no longer just an emotion but a lifestyle, marking a new era in its history.

While those bits of advice were being written on walls in March 2016, a group of marketing experts was gathering at the cultural festival SXSW for what was being called a "happiness intervention." Executives from companies including Walt Disney Imagineering and Soul

Cycle were part of a panel there titled "Designing Happiness," with the goal to identify "happiness trigger moments." Attendees were eager to learn how to create such moments via their own brands, already convinced that happiness was perhaps the ultimate selling proposition.[47] The Pennsylvania tourism office apparently thought so when it decided in 2016 that its new marketing slogan would be "Pursue Your Happiness." The borrowing of Jefferson's phrase represented "a powerful marketing platform that will inspire travelers to explore the commonwealth while on their personal pursuit of happiness," said Carrie Fisher Lepore, Deputy Secretary, Office of Marketing, Tourism and Film, thinking the Keystone State had plenty to make tourists happy. With research showing that among tourists "the overarching motivator is happiness," the tourism office also decided to call its travel guide *Happy Traveler* and renamed its e-newsletter "Happy Thoughts."[48]

Seemingly reaching the same conclusion that happiness was "the overarching motivator" to consumer behavior, marketers in many product and service categories looked for every opportunity to link their brands to it. That same year, for example, Booking.com commissioned research showing that almost half of those surveyed felt that traveling somewhere on vacation brought them more happiness than what they experienced on their wedding day (29 percent believed that taking a vacation offered more happiness than having a baby, rather sadly). "People can boost their happiness in a few simple clicks on Booking.com," said David Mau, director of product for the most popular hotel reservation website in the world.[49] Not to be outdone, StubHub, the largest ticket marketplace in the world, used findings from its study showing that it was attending live events that "held the keys to happiness." Live events like concerts were typically social and emotional experiences that created lasting memories, StubHub maintained, its research confirming that personal happiness was most likely to result from spending meaningful time with others.[50]

LG's "Experience Happiness" initiative serves as another example of how corporations have appropriated happiness as a marketing tool. In 2017, the giant electronics company launched a corporate social responsibility program called "Life's Good: Experience Happiness" targeted to young Americans. "LG's Experience Happiness program is working with partners to bring scientific insights and tools for sustainable happiness to America's youth, to help make life good for generations to come," William Cho, president and CEO, announced. Those partners were the Greater Good Science Center (GGSC) based at the University of California, Berkeley ("the epicenter for research on happiness and gratitude," according to the *New York Times*) and Inner Explorer, which brought mindfulness into school curricula across the country. With research showing that two of three young people were "stressed," teaching them "happiness skills" like mindfulness would help them recognize that life was good, a seamless blend of positive psychology, do-goodism, and corporate branding.[51]

Not just huge corporations but startups like nakedmoment.com are committed to bringing happiness to us all. The bold mission of the website is "to raise happiness in the US, and worldwide," Naked Moment states, its pair of millennial cofounders believing that "we all have the right to be happy, and being happy will not only benefit you personally, but everyone around you as well." Visitors to the website are welcome to sample a free Happiness Formula training program described as "a step-by-step guide that leads you down the trail of happiness and gives you the tools to take action in your own life" (a "30-day happiness money back guarantee" is offered to unsatisfied customers of the complete program).[52] Needless to say, some consumers do not appreciate Corporate America's strategic deployment of happiness. "Now my health care plan is spamming me with HappyTalk," complained Alex Beam of the *Boston Globe* after he received in the mail a brochure called "Eight Satisfying Secrets of Happy People." Among United Healthcare's secrets to "cultivate more happiness in your life" were "Look on the brighter side," a nice idea perhaps but not all what would actually make Beam happy—the costs of his premium and deductible being lowered.[53]

The Building Blocks of Happiness

With the happiness movement now a major feature of everyday life in America, it is not surprising that many of those in the public sector are thinking long and hard about what role the government should play in people's lives. Taking inspiration from countries including Bhutan, Dubai, and the United Arab Republic, which have appointed ministers of happiness, more local communities across the country are exploring how they should best approach the well-being of their citizens. Somerville, Massachusetts (a Boston suburb), Aspen, Colorado, and Santa

Monica, California, are recent additions to the growing list of communities attempting to determine how happy their respective residents are and what elected officials might do to make them happier. It's debatable whether happiness should be part of the political arena, of course, but it seems clear that government at all levels will take a greater interest in that dimension of people's lives in the future.[54]

The halo effect of the World Happiness Report (which is released annually on the International Day of Happiness) has much to do with local politicians' concern about their constituency's relative state of emotional well-being. If money and the things it can buy do not produce happiness, as most of the research done in the area suggests, one does have to wonder if economics should serve as the best measure of the health of society (a 2017 study found that people who bought "time" with money—that is, paid people for services they would otherwise do—did become somewhat happier).[55] The authors of the report go much further than ranking the relative happiness of countries (now up to 155) by directly challenging what it calls "the tyranny of GDP." Rather than gross domestic product, as tiny Bhutan concluded decades ago, it should be happiness by which governments should base how well citizens are doing and being served, the Sustainable Development Solutions Network, along with the UN and the Ernesto Illy Foundation, maintain. More nations are taking heed of such insight. "Happiness is increasingly considered the proper measure of social progress and the goal of public policy," the latest report reads, cause for concern among those thinking that government should stick to economics. "The Declaration of Independence does say that the 'pursuit of happiness' is one of the rights that government must secure for us," observed Gene Epstein in *Barron's* in 2017, "but how we pursue it is our own business, and how we define happiness is our own affair."[56]

Given how passionate each side feels about the issue, a war over how taxpayer money is used may be looming as laissez-faire capitalists battle it out with those who believe that findings of the World Happiness Report are valid. "Measuring self-reported happiness and achieving well-being should be on every nation's agenda as they begin to pursue the Sustainable Development Goals [SDGs]," said Jeffrey Sachs, the report's coeditor and director of the Earth Institute at Columbia University, making his case for "a holistic approach [toward policy making] that combines economic, social and environmental objectives." The United States had gotten much richer over the course of the last half-century but no happier, he added, prime evidence that economic growth should not be the nation's sole focus.[57] Rather, it was health, well-being, reduced inequalities, and climate action that were "the building blocks of happiness," urging more Americans to subscribe to these SDGs.[58]

Not surprisingly, the media made much of the fact that the United States had again not made the top ten list of happiest countries on the 2017 World Happiness Report. Even worse news was that the country received its lowest happiness score in a decade on the Gallup International Cantril ladder, more evidence that Americans were not succeeding in their long pursuit. "The United States can and should raise happiness by addressing America's multi-faceted social crisis—rising inequality, corruption, isolation, and distrust," Sachs had written in the report, hoping such research would steer policymakers away from their fixation on economic growth.[59] With Norway, Denmark, Iceland, Switzerland, and Finland finishing in the report's top five that year, it was easy for Sachs to conclude that social democracies that provided free or nearly free health care, higher education, and child support and a full year off for parental leave made people happy. Again, it was the SDGs (which were first proposed in 2015 as the means to bring about widespread peace and prosperity by 2030) that offered Americans the best chance of raising their level of happiness to that of citizens of these Northern European countries.[60]

The UN's sponsorship of both the World Happiness Report and the International Day of Happiness offered the organization a significantly higher public profile than that as a not very effective mediator of world peace. One wouldn't think of the UN as a particularly sophisticated marketer, but in promoting its Happiness Day in 2017 the global organization appeared to be taking a cue from corporations that were cleverly selling happiness to consumers. Adding some marketing spin to its rather wonky-sounding SDGs, the UN launched a "Small Smurfs, Big Goals" campaign on March 20 at its headquarters in New York. All the stars from the recently released *Smurfs: The Lost Village* movie were there, including Demi Lovato (Smurfette), Joe Manganiello (Hefty), and Mandy Patinkin (Papa Smurf). "This inspirational campaign highlights the fact that each and every one of us, no matter how young or old, small or big, can make our world a happier place," said Cristina Gallach, the UN's under secretary general for communications and the

Department of Public Information. At the same time in Belgium (home of the artist Peyo, who created the diminutive blue characters), a trio of Smurfs visited two elementary schools, with children responding with a loud "Yes" when asked if they were happy.[61]

As children around the world are taught a new narrative of happiness grounded in the ideals of wellness and sustainability, both for themselves and the planet as a whole, it is clear that we are entering another era in the history of the subject. The "subjective state of well-being" is rapidly evolving into a politically charged international movement freighted with important social and economic consequences that will likely impact the lives of people for generations to come. While the words are in our official charter, Americans have never held an exclusive claim on the pursuit of happiness, of course, but Jefferson's pithy phrase is well on the way to morphing into a global anthem and taking on meanings that go far beyond the emotional condition of an individual.

As these macro forces further spread, the problem of finding personal happiness remains, particularly for Americans, whose expectations for it have always exceeded the realities. Despite the abundance of research showing that significantly changing one's happiness quotient is an uphill battle, Americans are as committed to the fight as ever. "Happyism" (i.e., the study of and struggle for happiness) is today an immense field offering a seemingly endless stream of theories and therapies targeted to consumers seeking help or at least answers. Happy people live longer, some studies show, reason enough why the subject of happiness should be taken seriously. Still, Americans may be more interested in pursuing happiness than actually realizing it, one might conclude after examining its history over the last century, the journey deemed more fulfilling than the destination. Until we are genetically programmed to be happy, however, many of us will continue to chase after what is one of life's most desired states of being, with the future of happiness in America being no doubt a fascinating one.

EPILOGUE

Do we know any more about happiness in America after traveling through a century of its history? It's admittedly hard to say; the slipperiness of the subject that so many writers have confronted over the years has certainly informed this work. Given that some of the most brilliant minds since antiquity have struggled with understanding the nature of happiness, and even defining the term, it's not surprising that no single revelation toward achieving it has popped off these pages. Happiness is an emotion, first of all, and one of the more ambiguous ones, making it difficult if not impossible to realize it simply because one desires to. Adding to the problematic nature of happiness in America has been the fact that research in the field has been for the most part unreliable, a function of the major challenges involved in measuring and describing the emotion, whether on an individual or a collective basis. Still, my hope is that this book has contributed at least a little more to our general knowledge of happiness, and that readers have gained some insight into how the emotion operates within their own unique cognitive ecosystem.

Despite the major obstacles facing those wanting to be happier, many Americans have of course pursued it with considerable vigor. The gap between the desire for greater happiness and the finding of it has caused much frustration and consternation over the past century, a failure of sorts that continues to this day. The Founding Fathers' decision to include "the pursuit of happiness" as one of Americans' unalienable rights laid the foundation for what would turn out to be an ambitious and largely unsuccessful effort that this work has thoroughly documented, sometimes in painful detail. If there's one conclusion to make, it's that it is hard to be bullish on the future of happiness in America, with no amount of social, economic, or political engineering to likely reverse what appears to be a fundamental trait (and I believe flaw) in our national character. The emergence of a happiness movement powered by "positive psychology" represents the most direct and grandest attempt to enable people to be happier but, again, I'm personally not of the persuasion that any significant degree of any emotion can be concocted or conjured up by self-determination and/or -discipline.

Just to be clear, I am by no means against happiness, but I do think it is an overrated emotion, and one that has received much more attention than it probably deserves, especially in America over the past century. Any number of pursuits, particularly those that are aimed at improving the lives of others, I contend based on the evidence presented in this book, are more worthwhile than devoting much of one's time and energy trying to find happiness. During my own years of chasing happiness (and realizing a good deal of it), I remained consciously aware that I was skating the surface of life, and that I never felt fully engaged in the human experience. In short, being happy is a terrific ride but not the final stop on life's journey, I've come to conclude, reason for those who dare to keep going to the end of the emotional line.

To that point, I suggest that individuals seeking greater happiness should seriously consider abandoning that persistently losing proposition for one that is not only more realizable but one that I believe to be more emotionally fulfilling. In the preface to this book I made a distinction between happiness and joy, an idea that warrants further examination. Along the lines of what Anthony Seldon proposed in his *Beyond Happiness*, which I think is the best book on the subject, my advice is to shift one's emotional dynamic from happiness to joy (the subtitle of his book is "The Trap of Happiness and How to Find Deeper Meaning and Joy," probably the smartest sentence in these pages). While history clearly shows that attempting to attain happiness is at best an uphill battle, infusing one's life with greater joy is an entirely doable and I would argue a much nobler pursuit. Seldon did just that in his own life and so did I, and we are each the better person for it.[1]

Here then as an alternative to yet another recipe for happiness are what I propose to be the twelve essential ingredients of joy. (Todd Kashdan has also wisely suggested that bypassing happiness for a different course in life makes a lot of sense.) Because I equate joy with the degree to which one has developed as a human being, one can also think of these personality markers as "The Twelve Habits of Highly Evolved People." Listing a dozen pithy attributes obviously does not do justice to the enormity of the subject but is I believe a worthwhile exercise given how many of us are searching for greater meaning and purpose in life. Not attempting to put forth a kind of template for joy would represent a missed opportunity, as it is clear that Americans are avidly, perhaps desperately searching for deeper and richer emotional experiences. Use the following entirely subjective, in-no-particular-order observations if and as you'd like.

1. Positivism. Optimism—accentuating the positive and eliminating the negative, if you like—has always been strongly correlated with high levels of both happiness and joy. Seeing the glass half full rather than half empty, to use another cliché, is vital to maintaining the most basic rule of life: that it is worth living.
2. Purpose. A good reason to get up in the morning goes a long way to being a joyful person. Having a sense of direction, the setting and reaching of goals, and taking pride in accomplishments are all woven into the fabric of joy.
3. Presentism. Living as much as possible in the moment, rather than dwelling on the past or worrying about the future, is a guiding principle of joy. Today is infinitely more valuable than yesterday or tomorrow, making those living in the now much more likely to be joyful than those thinking about what might have been or what might be.
4. Realism. Regular reality checks help one manage one's expectations and keep the ups and downs of life in perspective, each things that joyful people tend to do. As well, accepting the truth that unhappiness is an essential part of life is ironically one of the keys to joy.
5. Appreciation. Taking pleasure in and being grateful for what one has chases away common scourges of unhappiness like envy and

disappointment. Comparing oneself (or one's stuff) to others is a road better not taken, as is attempting to "have it all" as there is no all to have.

6. Humbleness. Being fully aware of your limitations is oddly enough a prime way to feel really good about yourself. The most joyful people on Earth also happen to be the most modest, something a few world leaders might keep in mind.

7. Kindness. Adopting a philosophy of and approach to life simply around being kind is a powerful source of joy for oneself and others. Buddhism is heavily steeped in the idea of compassion, and it is hard to argue with joyful-as-all-get-out monks and the Dalai Lama.

8. Generosity. Enabling the well-being of friends, family, and complete strangers has proven to be a winning formula of personal joyfulness. Giving is a more rewarding experience than receiving, folk wisdom borne out by study after study.

9. Patience. An awareness of the vicissitudes of time and the imperfections within us all serves as a valuable tool in achieving joy. Life is about the means rather than the ends, something we tend to forget while we're scurrying around to get things done.

10. Curiosity. Viewing life as an endless opportunity to learn and/or experience things is a literally wonderful path to joy. Preserving at least a little of the child within is for me a very much underrated thing to do.

11. Faith. Not just the belief in a higher power but a view that there is some kind of grand design or order to the universe is integral to joy. Some perfectly content people may see life as a random series of acts but for my money embracing the idea that there is something bigger than oneself adds a whole other level to our limited time here.

12. Love. I'm convinced that filling one's life with as much love as possible is the ultimate avenue to joy. And, I might add, the love you take is equal to the love you make, as nice a way as any to end our story.

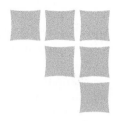

NOTES

Introduction

1. Darrin M. McMahon, *Happiness: A History* (New York: Atlantic Monthly Press, 2005); Nicholas P. White, *A Brief History of Happiness* (Hoboken, NJ: Wiley-Blackwell, 2006); Sissela Bok, *Exploring Happiness: From Aristotle to Brain Science* (New Haven, CT: Yale University Press, 2010).

2. Matthieu Ricard, *Happiness: A Guide to Developing Life's Most Important Skill* (New York: Little Brown, 2006); Gretchen Rubin, *The Happiness Project: Or, Why I Spent a Year Trying to Sing in the Morning, Clean My Closets, Fight Right, Read Aristotle, and Generally Have More Fun* (New York: Harper, 2009); Neil Pasricha, *The Happiness Equation: Want Nothing + Do Anything = Have Everything* (New York: G. P. Putnam's Sons, 2016).

3. Alain de Botton, *Status Anxiety* (New York: Pantheon, 2004).

4. worldhappiness.report.

5. House Minority Leader Nancy Pelosi (D-California) frequently remarked that the Affordable Care Act (Obamacare) was about "life, liberty and the pursuit of happiness," a classic example of the politicizing of the phrase. Kelly Cohen, "Pelosi: Obamacare Leads to 'Life, Liberty and the Pursuit of Happiness,'" *The Examiner*, March 23, 2016.

6. Lawrence R. Samuel, *The American Dream: A Cultural History* (Syracuse, NY: Syracuse University Press, 2012); Lawrence R. Samuel, *The American Way of Life: A Cultural History* (Madison, NJ: Fairleigh Dickinson University Press, 2017).

7. Lawrence R. Samuel, *The American Middle Class: A Cultural History* (New York: Routledge, 2013).

8. L. H. Butterfield, "But What Is Happiness?" *New York Times*, May 3, 1953, BR16.

9. Andrew Delbanco, "Are You Happy Yet?" *New York Times Sunday Magazine*, May 7, 2000, SM44.

10. Robert Darnton, "The Pursuit of Happiness," *Wilson Quarterly*, Autumn 1995, 42; the Scottish-Irish philosopher Francis Hutcheson also likely served as inspiration for Jefferson.

11. Butterfield, "But What Is Happiness?"

12. Jeffrey Kluger, Alex Aciman, and Katy Steinmetz, "The Happiness of Pursuit," *Time*, July 8, 2013, 24.

13. Jon Meacham, "Free to Be Happy," *Time*, July 8, 2103, 38; see Garry Wills's *Inventing America: Jefferson's Declaration of Independence* (New York: Doubleday, 1978) for much more on the role of happiness in the Declaration of Independence.

14. William V. Shannon, "What Is Happiness?" *New York Times*, July 5, 1976, 11.

15. Timothy J. Shannon, "America: Pursuing Happiness Since 1776," *Valley News*, July 4, 2016, 6.

16. Publius, "The Pursuit of Happiness," *The New Leader*, October 5, 1987, 12.

17. Charles Murray, *In Pursuit of Happiness and Good Government* (New York: Simon & Schuster, 1988) 6.

18. Peter N. Stearns, "The History of Happiness," *Harvard Business Review*, January–February 2012.

19. "The History of Happiness."

Chapter 1

1. "Seeks to Protect Term 'Happiness,'" *New York Times*, February 10, 1928, 32.

2. M. Nicholson, "Are We a Happy People?" *Harper's*, December 1922, 38.

3. T. L. Masson, "New Roads to Happiness," *World's Work*, July 1922, 256.

4. "Happiness Surveys Asked for Schools," *New York Times*, January 2, 1922, 17.

5. Lawrence R. Samuel, *Supernatural America: A Cultural History* (Westport, CT: Praeger, 2011).

6. "Asserts He Holds Key to Happiness," *New York Times*, November 5, 1923, 6.

7. "Asserts He Holds Key to Happiness."

8. "Go to Hear Rawson, Find Healer Dead," *New York Times*, November 12, 1923, 36.

9. Lawrence R. Samuel, *Shrink: A Cultural History of Psychoanalysis in America* (Lincoln: University of Nebraska Press, 2013).

10. "Town Hall Filled with Coue Lecture," *New York Times*, January 16, 1924, 17.

11. "Finds Same Griefs Hit Rich and Poor," *New York Times*, February 2, 1925, 9.

12. Evans Clark, "Happiness and Personal Income Are Not Entire Strangers," *New York Times*, May 3, 1925, BR10.

13. "Feminism Blights Woman's Happiness," *New York Times*, December 1926, E12.

14. "Feminism Blights Woman's Happiness."

15. Corra Harris, "I—Antiquated Happiness," *Forum*, December 1928, 816.

16. Dora Russell, "II—The Vices of Victorian Virtues," *Forum*, December 1928, 811.

17. "Women Debate Value of Work Outside Home," *New York Times*, March 26, 1929, 39.

18. "Petting Cuts Happiness," *New York Times*, December 4, 1926, 2.

19. "Every-Day Psychology," *New York Times*, November 14, 1926, BR20.

20. "Chemists of World to Meet on July 4," *New York Times*, June 19, 1927, E9.

21. "Two Philosophers Debate Democracy," *New York Times*, October 23, 1927, 12.

22. "Dr. Krass Says Balance Is Basis of Happiness; Calls It a Harmony of Mind, Body and Soul," *New York Times*, December 30, 1929, 18.

23. "Emphasizes Value of Mental Health," *New York Times*, November 15, 1929, 23.

24. Bruce Rae, "Personality Put Under Microscope," *New York Times*, September 4, 1929, 4; "What's in Happiness Tested at Columbia," *New York Times*, March 9, 1930, 153.

25. Florence Finch Kelly, "Happiness Viewed as a Possible Science," *New York Times*, October 20, 1929, BR7.

26. Kelly, "Happiness Viewed as a Possible Science."

27. V. F. Calverton, "What Is Happiness?" *The Nation*, December 25, 1929, 778.

28. "What Is Happiness?" *Forum*, January 1929, XXXVII.

29. "What Is Happiness?"

30. Rose C. Feld, "Bertrand Russell in Quest of the Key to Happiness," *New York Times*, October 19, 1930, 61.

31. W. B. Curry, "Why Are We Unhappy?" *New Republic*, December 3, 1930, 80.

32. Henry Hazlitt, "The Art of Being Happy," *The Nation*, October 8, 1930, 379.

33. "American Happiness," *New York Times*, June 11, 1931, 24.

34. "Dr. Adler Deplores Hunt for Happiness," *New York Times*, May 11, 1931, 14.

35. "Fosdick Asserts 'Futilism' Is Rife," *New York Times*, January 6, 1930, 38.

36. "Happiness Einstein Creed," *New York Times*, October 14, 1931, 25.

37. Dr. Albert Einstein, "They Say," *New York Times*, February 22, 1931, 109.

38. "Denies Machine Age Adds to Happiness," *New York Times*, July 12, 1931, N3.

39. "Better Times Due, Schwab Declares," *New York Times*, December 20, 1931, N8.

40. "Happiness Test Given to 500 Men," *New York Times*, July 13, 1931, 17.

41. "Asks 25-Hour Week to Save the Church," *New York Times*, October 17, 1932, 13.

42. "Decries False Ideal," *New York Times*, February 17, 1933, 14.

43. "Dr. Goodspeed's Aids to Contentment," *New York Times*, March 26, 1933, BR10.

44. "Hunt for Happiness Held to Be Futile," *New York Times*, January 2, 1933, 26.

45. "Tahiti's Self-Governing Lepers Attain a Measure of Happiness," *New York Times*, November 19, 1933, XX8.

46. Louis Berg, "The Quest for Happiness," in *The Human Personality* (Upper Saddle River, NJ: Prentice Hall/Pearson Education, 1933), 283.

47. Berg, "The Quest for Happiness."

48. "Wife-Ruled Homes Held Least Happy," *New York Times*, June 28, 1934, 25.

49. "Marriage & Happiness," *Time*, October 17, 1938, 59.

50. Bell Wiley, *So You're Going to Get Married* (Philadelphia, PA: J. B. Lippincott & Company, 1938); I. M. Hotep, *Love and Happiness* (New York: Alfred A. Knopf, 1938).

51. Harold L. Ickes, "Where Is the Nation Heading?" *New York Times*, May 27, 1934, SM1.

52. "Roosevelts Note Cheer," *New York Times*, December 29, 1934, 13.

53. "Dr. Cadman's Talks," *New York Times*, November 24, 1935, BR12.

54. "Is Everybody Happy?" *Saturday Evening Post*, November 30, 1935, 22.

55. "Dr. Cadman's Talks."

56. Rose C. Feld, "A Physician's Prescription for Finding Happiness," *New York Times*, September 22, 1935, BR13.

57. P. H., "Mr. Powys Charts the Art of Happiness," *New York Times*, May 5, 1935, BR9.

58. "A Primer to Happiness," *New York Times*, December 22, 1935, BR13.

59. "The Secret of Happiness," *New York Times*, September 8, 1935, E8.

60. "The Secret of Happiness."

61. "Toward Happiness," *New York Times*, November 15, 1936, BR26.

62. "Miscellaneous Book Reviews," *New York Times*, September 19, 1937, 112.

63. "Marston Advises 3 Ls for Success," *New York Times*, November 11, 1937, 27.

64. "Personal Happiness Rules Study Courses," *New York Times*, November 19, 1939, D5.

Chapter 2

1. "Happiness Is First in High School Poll," *New York Times*, December 5, 1945, 22.

2. A. M. Pleslak, "The Paradox of Happiness," *Catholic World*, November 1953, 86–91.

3. M. Konroff, "For Happiness, Take a Step Down," *Good Housekeeping*, April 1943, 37.

4. Alan M. Winkler, *Home Front U.S.A.: America during World War II* (Wheeling, IL: Harlan Davidson, 2012), 105.

5. "$1,589,289 Asked in Hospital Drive," *New York Times*, October 22, 1940, 28.

6. "World Happiness Nazi Aim, Says Ley," *New York Times*, May 15, 1940, 5.

7. "Knudsen Warns on Readjustment," *New York Times*, November 12, 1944, 40.

8. Morris L. Kaplan, "Scholars See Peril in Greatest 'Crisis,'" *New York Times*, August 27, 1945, 21.

9. Martin Gumpert, "Research in Happiness," *Nation*, August 17, 1946, 185.

10. "Happiness Called Democracy's Goal," *New York Times*, October 2, 1947, 27.

11. Harry M. Davis, "Health and Happiness," *New York Times*, February 2, 1947, BR21.

12. Davis, "Health and Happiness."

13. Lucy Freeman, "Courses Suggested in Human Relationships," *New York Times*, July 28, 1948, 25.

14. William F. Ogburn, "Can Science Bring Us Happiness?" *New York Times Sunday Magazine*, December 4, 1949, SM14.

15. Russell W. Davenport, "A *Life* Round Table on the Pursuit of Happiness," *Life*, July 12, 1948, 95.

16. Davenport, "A *Life* Round Table on the Pursuit of Happiness."

17. Davenport, "A *Life* Round Table on the Pursuit of Happiness."

18. Davenport, "A *Life* Round Table on the Pursuit of Happiness."

19. Luther Conant, "Ten-Day Plan for Happiness," *Woman's Home Companion*, October 1950, 11; Davenport, "A *Life* Round Table on the Pursuit of Happiness."

20. B. Benson, "What Makes People Happy?" *Ladies' Home Journal*, September 1946, 26; L. Chase, "Happy Heart," *Vogue*, December 1956, 113.

21. M. R. Johnstone, "Happiness Is Where You Are," *Better Homes & Gardens*, May 1957, 262.

22. Fredric Wertham, "Short-Cut to Joy," *The Saturday Review of Literature*, April 22, 1950, 21.

23. James Gordan Gilkey, *Here Is Help for You* (New York: Macmillan, 1951); Norman Vincent Peale, *The Power of Positive Thinking* (New York: Prentice-Hall, 1952). See also Fulton J. Sheen's *Way to Happiness: A Guide to Peace, Hope and*

Contentment (Garden City, NY: Garden City Books, 1954), and Billy Graham's *The Secret of Happiness* (New York: Doubleday, 1955).

24. Lin Yutang, "Do American Writers Shun Happiness?" *The Saturday Review of Literature*, July 15, 1950, 7.

25. Yutang, "Do American Writers Shun Happiness?"

26. Erich Fromm, *The Sane Society* (New York: Rinehart and Company, 1955).

27. S. Stylites, "All Aboard for Happiness!" *Christian Century*, August 13, 1952, 919.

28. John Crosby, "Dash of Humor Suggested to Brighten TV 'Cavalcade,'" *The Hartford Courant*, January 12, 1953, 6.

29. "Rockefeller Gives Happiness Formula," *New York Times*, June 24, 1951, 50.

30. "Happiness Called a Right and a Duty," *New York Times*, December 29, 1952, 20.

31. Jane Cobb, "The Woman in the Case," *New York Times*, May 25, 1952, BR22.

32. Cobb, "The Woman in the Case."

33. Bernice Fitz-Gibbon, "Woman in the *Gay* Flannel Suit," *New York Times*, January 29, 1956, 196.

34. Joseph Wood Krutch, "Old Truths Newly Said," *New York Times*, October 16, 1955, BR45.

35. Donald Harrington, "New Light on an Old Adventure," *The Saturday Review of Literature*, October 8, 1955, 12.

36. Bertrand Russell, "The American Way (A Briton Says) Is Dour," *New York Times Sunday Magazine*, June 15, 1952, SM12.

37. Russell, "The American Way (A Briton Says) Is Dour."

38. Russell, "The American Way (A Briton Says) Is Dour."

39. Russell, "The American Way (A Briton Says) Is Dour."

40. Sukich Nimmanheminda, "A Thai's Formula for Happiness," *New York Times Sunday Magazine*, December 2, 1956, SM52.

41. Nimmanheminda, "A Thai's Formula for Happiness."

42. Robert K. Plumb, "Psychiatry Upset by 'Peace' Drugs," *New York Times*, July 6, 1956, 23.

43. Wertham, "Short-Cut to Joy."

44. Plumb, "Psychiatry Upset by 'Peace' Drugs."

45. Jess Raley, "That Wonderful Frustrated Feeling," *The American Mercury*, July 1957, 20.

46. Robert G. Whalen, "I Quit!" *New York Times Sunday Magazine*, May 19, 1957, SM24.

47. "TV Film Omission Irks Convention," *New York Times*, August 14, 1956, 13.

48. "TV Film Omission Irks Convention."

49. Jack Gould, "TV: C.B.S. Outsmarted," *New York Times*, August 14, 1956, 53.

50. Russell Baker, "President Finishes 5-Day Tour; He Finds the Nation Prosperous," *New York Times*, October 21, 1956, 70.

51. Anna Petersen, "Sandburg Notes Prosperity Peril," *New York Times*, April 17, 1956, 33.

52. George P. Elliott, "The Happiness Rat Race," *The Nation*, October 3, 1959, 190.

53. James Truslow Adams, "America Faces 1933's Realities," *New York Times Sunday Magazine*, January 1, 1933, SM1.

54. John F. Bridge, "The Contented Americans," *Wall Street Journal*, May 21, 1959, 12.

55. Bridge, "The Contented Americans."

Chapter 3

1. "Lag in Happiness Found Among Young Today," *New York Times*, October 14, 1979, 39.

2. F. L. Lucas, "Party of One," *Holiday*, August 1960, 9.

3. John E. Gibson, "Your Chances for Happiness," *Science Digest*, January 1961, 9.

4. Gibson, "Your Chances for Happiness."

5. Gibson, "Your Chances for Happiness."

6. Gibson, "Your Chances for Happiness."

7. "What Makes You Happy?" *Science Digest*, October 1963, 36.

8. "What Makes You Happy?"

9. "What Makes You Happy?"

10. "What Makes You Happy?" *Changing Times*, November 1963, 31.

11. June Callwood, *Love, Hate, Fear, Anger and the Other Lively Emotions* (New York: Doubleday, 1964); L. J. Hurley, "Happiness Is a Journey," *Farm Journal*, July 1964, 43.

12. Joseph Wood Krutch, "Through Happiness with Slide Rule and Calipers," *Saturday Review*, November 2, 1963, 12.

13. Krutch, "Through Happiness with Slide Rule and Calipers."

14. John Ciardi, "Is Everybody Happy?" *Saturday Review*, March 14, 1964, 18.

15. Ciardi, "Is Everybody Happy?"

16. Seymour Topping, "Peking Discounts Comforts of Life," *New York Times*, July 17, 1964, 5.

17. Ian Stewart, "Happiness (Says Mao) Is a Hard Day's Work," *New York Times*, September 27, 1964, SM34.

18. Donald D. Barry and Carol Barner Barry, "Happiness Is Driving Your Own Moskvich," *New York Times*, April 10, 1966, 185.

19. Russell Baker, "Observer: Happiness Goes to Washington," *New York Times*, August 12, 1965, 26.

20. Baker, "Observer: Happiness Goes to Washington."

21. John Herbers, "Kennedy Attacks Humphrey Appeal," *New York Times*, May 16, 1968, 20.

22. Roy Reed, "Humphrey Is Stung by Attacks on His 'Politics of Happiness,'" *New York Times*, May 25, 1968, 9.

23. Russell Baker, "Observer: The Politics of Happiness," *New York Times*, April 30, 1968, 46.

24. Philip H. Dougherty, "Advertising: Happiness Is the Way at T.W.A.," *New York Times*, March 24, 1969, 68.

25. Philip H. Dougherty, "Advertising: B.B.D.O.'s Happiness Profile," *New York Times*, March 9, 1972, 55.

26. Mildred Newman and Bernard Berkowitz, *How to Be Your Own Best Friend* (New York: Random House, 1971).

27. Paul Cameron, "3 Faces of Happiness," *Psychology Today*, August 1974, 63.

28. "Jefferson's Artful Dodger," *Psychology Today*, October 1975, 66.

29. "Jefferson's Artful Dodger."

30. Phillip Shaver and Jonathan Freedman, "Your Pursuit of Happiness," *Psychology Today*, August 1976, 26.

31. Shaver and Freedman, "Your Pursuit of Happiness."

32. Shaver and Freedman, "Your Pursuit of Happiness."

33. Jack Horn, "Love: The Most Important Ingredient in Happiness," *Psychology Today*, July 1976, 98.

34. "Pursuit of Happiness: Rite of Infinite Variety," *New York Times*, July 3, 1976, 47.

35. "Pursuit of Happiness: Rite of Infinite Variety."

36. "Pursuit of Happiness: Rite of Infinite Variety."

37. Samuel Walton, "Happiness: Who's Got It? How You Can Get It!" *Saturday Evening Post*, September 1977, 50.

38. Jack Horn, "Fulfillment—It Requires Balanced Satisfactions," *Psychology Today*, September 1977, 33.

39. Jonathan Freedman, "Happy People," *Family Health*, August 1978, 30.

40. Freedman, "Happy People."

41. Freedman, "Happy People."

42. Freedman, "Happy People."

43. Freedman, "Happy People."

44. Freedman, "Happy People."

45. Frank Trippett, "The Scientific Pursuit of Happiness," *Time*, March 19, 1979, 100.

46. Johannes Eff, "Your Erroneous Bones," *National Review*, March 2, 1979, 298.

47. Trippett, "The Scientific Pursuit of Happiness."

48. Trippett, "The Scientific Pursuit of Happiness."

49. Trippett, "The Scientific Pursuit of Happiness."

50. Gail Sheehy, "Introducing the Postponing Generation," *Esquire*, October 1979, 29.

51. Trippett, "The Scientific Pursuit of Happiness."

52. Trippett, "The Scientific Pursuit of Happiness."

Chapter 4

1. Bill Barol, "Put on a Happy Face . . . Or Else," *Newsweek*, February 29, 1989, 74.

2. Barol, "Put on a Happy Face . . . Or Else."

3. Andrew M. Greeley, "The State of the Nation's Happiness," *Psychology Today*, January 1981, 14–16.

4. Robert Coles, "Happiness," *Vogue*, January 1983, 204.

5. Taki Theodoracopulos, "Unending Bliss," *Esquire*, August 1983, 121.

6. Theodoracopulos, "Unending Bliss."

7. Paul L. Wachtel, *The Poverty of Affluence: A Psychological Portrait of the American Way of Life* (New York: Free Press, 1983).

8. Anthony Brandt, "In Selfish Pursuit," *Esquire*, March 1984, 20–21.

9. B. Simmons, "Happiness Anxiety," *Mademoiselle*, June 1983, 154.

10. Lesley Hazleton, "What's Good About Feeling Bad," *Vogue*, September 1984, 800.

11. Hazleton, "What's Good About Feeling Bad."

12. "Happiness: How Americans Pursue It," *U.S. News & World Report*, March 4, 1985, 60.

13. "Happiness: How Americans Pursue It."

14. Joan Juliet Buck, "Gluttons for Happiness," *Vogue*, December 1984, 132.

15. J. R. Freeland, "The First Addiction—Happiness," *USA Today*, September 1986, 62.

16. Harold Kushner, *When All You've Ever Wanted Isn't Enough: The Search for a Life That Matters* (New York: Summit Books, 1986).

17. Alvin P. Sanoff, "Happiness: How Americans Pursue It; A Personal Quest," *U.S. News & World Report*, March 4, 1985, 63; Gordon Witkin, "Happiness: How Americans Pursue It; Back to Nature," *U.S. News & World Report*, March 4, 1985, 64.

18. Joseph Carey, "Happiness: How Americans Pursue It; Close to God," *U.S. News & World Report*, March 4, 1985, 67; Sarah Peterson, "Happiness: How Americans Pursue It; Thirst for Success," *U.S. News & World Report*, March 4, 1985, 61.

19. "Happiness: How Americans Pursue It."

20. Rae Ciorelli, "Get Happy," *Maclean's*, September 16, 1996, 54.

21. William H. Willimon, "Have a Happy Day," *The Christian Century*, March 19–26, 1986, 287.

22. Diane Swanbrow, "The Paradox of Happiness," *Psychology Today*, July/August 1989, 37.

23. Ardath Rodale, "Searching for the Light of Happiness," *Prevention*, October 1996, 168.

24. Swanbrow, "The Paradox of Happiness."

25. Swanbrow, "The Paradox of Happiness."

26. Alan Thein Durning, "Are We Happy Yet?" *Futurist*, January–February 1993, 21.

27. Robert E. Lane, "Does Money Buy Happiness?" *The Public Interest*, Fall 1993, 61.

28. David Gelman, "Counting Your Blessings," *Newsweek*, May 24, 1993, 57.

29. Nancy Wartik, "Is Everybody Happy?" *American Health*, May 1995, 38.

30. David G. Myers, "Pursuing Happiness," *Psychology Today*, July/August 1993, 32.

31. Ariane Barth, "Pursuing the Secret of Happiness," *World Press Review*, April 1993, 22.

32. Barth, "Pursuing the Secret of Happiness."

33. "The Road to Happiness," *Psychology Today*, July/August 1994, 32.

34. "The Road to Happiness."

35. Maggie Scarf, "The Happiness Syndrome," *The New Republic*, December 5, 1994, 25.

36. Scarf, "The Happiness Syndrome."

37. Peter Doskoch, "Mirth on Earth," *Psychology Today*, July/August 1995, 48–49.

38. Mark Epstein, "Opening Up to Happiness," *Psychology Today*, July/August 1995, 42.

39. Epstein, "Opening Up to Happiness."

40. Ciorelli, "Get Happy."

41. Ciorelli, "Get Happy."

42. Ciorelli, "Get Happy."

43. Dava Sobel, "Mihaly Csikszentmihalyi," *Omni*, January 1995, 73.

44. Mihaly Csikszentmihalyi, *Finding Flow* (New York: Basic Books, 1997).

45. Mihaly Csikszentmihalyi, "Happiness and Creativity: Going With the Flow," *Futurist*, September/October 1997, 8.

46. Csikszentmihalyi, "Happiness and Creativity: Going With the Flow."

47. Dan Seligman, "Does Money Buy Happiness?" *Forbes*, April 21, 1997, 394.

48. Edward Cornish, "Happiness and Wealth," *Futurist*, September/October 1997, 13.

49. "A Network of Friends Crucial for Happiness," *USA Today Magazine*, December 1998, 9.

50. Charles W. Anderson, "Chemical Dependency," *Vital Speeches of the Day*, August 15, 1999, 653.

51. Seligman, "Does Money Buy Happiness?"

52. David G. Myers and Ed Diener, "The Science of Happiness," *Futurist*, September/October 1997, 2.

53. Myers and Diener, "The Science of Happiness."

54. Dorothy Foltz-Gray, "My Happiness Gene," *Health*, September 1997, 60.

55. R. MacKenzie, "Will More Sleep Really Make Me Happier Than More Money?" *New Choices for Retirement Living*, November 1993, 96.

56. B. De Angelis, "Happiness Is . . . ," *Good Housekeeping*, October 1994, 72.

57. David G. Myers and Ed Diener, "Finding Happiness: Is It Just Avoiding Pain?" *Current*, November 1997, 3–7.

58. Foltz-Gray, "My Happiness Gene."

59. William J. O'Malley, "Happiness," *America*, May 9, 1998, 10–14.

60. Mark Kingwell, "Come on Get Happy," *Saturday Night*, March 1998, 46.

61. Katherine Marsh, "Jumping for Joy," *Good Housekeeping*, June 1999, 26.

Chapter 5

1. Jason Skog, "Beach Man Named Nation's Happiest," pilotonline.com, March 3, 2003.

2. Ann Japenga, "Dare To Be Happy," *Health*, May 2000, 120–24; R. McClory, "The Happiest Place on Earth (Hint: It's Not Disneyland)," *U.S. Catholic*, September 2000, 18.

3. Mark Lilla, "Ignorance and Bliss," *The Wilson Quarterly*, Summer 2001, 64–75.

4. Andrew Delbanco, "Are You Happy Yet?" *New York Times Sunday Magazine*, May 7, 2000, SM44.

5. Martha Beck, *Finding Your Own North Star: Claiming the Life You Were Meant to Live* (New York: MJF Books, 2001).

6. Ellen Welty, "The Girl You Used To Be," *Good Housekeeping*, February 2002, 74–77.

7. Ronald W. Dworkin, "The Medicalization of Unhappiness," *The Public Interest*, Summer 2001, 85–99. See also Dworkin's excellent *Artificial Happiness: The Dark Side of the New Happy Class* (New York: Carroll & Graf, 2006) for the historical roots of medicalized unhappiness.

8. Stephanie Dolgoff, "How Happy Are You This Minute?" *Glamour*, May 2002, 188–90.

9. Bonnie Friedman, "This Is It, My Pet Pachooch!" *O: The Oprah Magazine*, March 2006, 217–18.

10. Dan Baker, "Caught in the Happiness Trap?" *Prevention*, February 2003, 132–39.

11. Alison Stein Wellner and David Adox, "Happy Days," *Psychology Today*, May/June 2000, 32.

12. Delbanco, "Are You Happy Yet?"

13. Holly J. Morris, "Happiness Explained," *U.S. News & World Report*, September 3, 2001, 46.

14. Robert Epstein, "Happiness Reexamined," *Psychology Today*, January/February 2001, 7.

15. His Holiness the Dalai Lama and Howard C. Cutler, *The Art of Happiness: A Handbook for Living* (New York: Riverhead Books, 1998).

16. Steven Reiss, *Who Am I? The 16 Basic Desires That Motivate Our Happiness and Define Our Personalities* (New York: Tarcher/Putnam, 2000).

17. Martin Seligman, *Authentic Happiness: Using the New Positive Psychology to Realize Your Potential for Lasting Fulfillment* (New York: Free Press, 2002).

18. John H. Richardson, "Wheee!" *Esquire*, June 2002, 82.

19. Richard Corliss and David Bjerklie, "Is There a Formula for Joy?" *Time*, January 20, 2003, 72.

20. Corliss and Bjerklie, "Is There a Formula for Joy?"

21. Jon Gertner, "The Futile Pursuit of Happiness," *New York Times Sunday Magazine*, September 7, 2003, 44.

22. C. Coles, "Genetically Engineered Happiness," *The Futurist*, July/August 2003, 16.

23. "The Happiness Craze," *Tricycle*, Fall 2005, 64–86.

24. Richard A. Easterlin, "The Economics of Happiness," *Daedalus*, Spring 2004, 26.

25. Easterlin, "The Economics of Happiness."

26. Robert H. Frank, "How Not to Buy Happiness," *Daedalus*, Spring 2004, 69–79.

27. Robert Biswas-Diener, Ed Diener, and Maya Tamir, "The Psychology of Subjective Well-Being," *Daedalus*, Spring 2004, 18–25.

28. Chip Brown, "The (Scientific) Pursuit of Happiness," *Smithsonian*, May 2004, 102–8.

29. Brown, "The (Scientific) Pursuit of Happiness."

30. "Get Happy," *Time*, January 17, 2005, A1.

31. Michael D. Lemonick and Dan Cray, "The Biology of Joy," *Time*, January 17, 2005, A12–A17; Kristina Dell, "The Paths to Pleasure," *Time*, January 17, 2005, A19.

32. Carlin Flora, "Happy Hour," *Psychology Today*, January/February 2005, 45–46.

33. Kaja Perina, "Happiness: The Golden Mistake," *Psychology Today*, January/February 2005, 5.

34. Kathleen McGowan, "The Pleasure Paradox," *Psychology Today*, January/February 2005, 52.

35. McGowan, "The Pleasure Paradox."

36. "Eight Steps Toward a More Satisfying Life," *Time*, January 17, 2005, A8–A9.

37. Dell, "The Paths to Pleasure."

38. Lemonick and Cray, "The Biology of Joy."

39. Lemonick and Cray, "The Biology of Joy."

40. Deborah Kotz, "Get Happy, and You'll Live Longer," *U.S. News & World Report*, December 25, 2006, 48–49.

41. Walter Kirn, Nadia Mustafa, and Elizabeth Coady, "It's a Glad, Sad, Mad World," *Time*, January 17, 2005, A65–A67.

42. Cynthia G. Wagner, "The Well-Being of Nations," *The Futurist*, November–December 2006, 12.

43. Wagner, "The Well-Being of Nations."

44. Gregg Easterbrook, "The Real Truth about Money," *Time*, January 17, 2005, A32–A34.

45. Easterbrook, "The Real Truth about Money."

46. David Futrelle, "Can Money Buy Happiness?" *Money*, August 2006, 127.

47. Futrelle, "Can Money Buy Happiness?"

48. Cynthia G. Wagner, "How to Buy Happiness," *The Futurist*, September–October 2007, 6.

49. Jean Chatzky, "Shopping for Happiness? Here's What to Buy," *Money*, April 2007, 28.

50. D. T. Max, "Happiness 101," *New York Times Sunday Magazine*, January 7, 2007, 46–51.

51. Sharon Begley, "Happiness: Enough Already," *Newsweek*, February 11, 2008, 50–52.

52. Begley, "Happiness: Enough Already."

53. Begley, "Happiness: Enough Already."

54. Begley, "Happiness: Enough Already."

55. Jennifer Barrett, "The 'How To' of Leading a Happy Life," *Newsweek*, January 28, 2008, 60.

56. Alice Park, "The Happiness Effect," *Time*, December 22, 2008, 40–42.

57. Katha Pollitt, "Are You Happy?" *The Nation*, October 19, 2009, 10.

58. Pollitt, "Are You Happy?"

59. Pollitt, "Are You Happy?"

60. Carlin Flora, "The Pursuit of Happiness," *Psychology Today*, January/February 2009, 62.

61. Flora, "The Pursuit of Happiness."

62. Julia Baird, "Positively Downbeat," *Newsweek*, October 5, 2009, 26.

63. Walter Mosley, "Get Happy," *The Nation*, October 5, 2009, 23.

64. Cristian Samper, "GNP or GNH?" *Smithsonian*, May 2008, 36.

65. Richard Layard, *Happiness: Lessons from a New Science* (New York: Penguin, 2005).

66. Begley, "Happiness: Enough Already."

Chapter 6

1. M. L. H., "Seeking the Peak," *Psychology Today*, November/December 2010, 27.

2. Elizabeth Kolbert, "Everybody Have Fun," *New Yorker*, March 22, 2010, 72–74.

3. Kolbert, "Everybody Have Fun."

4. Michael I. Norton, "Yes, Money Can Buy Happiness," *Forbes*, September 13, 2010, 1.

5. Belinda Luscombe, "The Cost of Happiness," *Time*, September 27, 2010, 56.

6. Roya Wolverson, "Happy Money," *Time*, October 10, 2011, 40.

7. Timothy Renick, "Pursuing Happiness," *Christian Century*, January 11, 2011, 22–24.

8. Lauren Sandler, "The American Nightmare," *Psychology Today*, March/April 2011, 70–77.

9. Wesley J. Smith, "Get Happy!" *The Weekly Standard*, May 7, 2012, 25.

10. Smith, "Get Happy!"

11. Laura Musikanski and John de Graaf, "Surveying Happiness," *The Progressive*, August 2012, 26–27.

12. Deirdre N. McCloskey, "Happyism," *The New Republic*, June 28, 2012, 16–23.

13. Algis Valiunas, "Have Much, Want Much," *Commentary*, September 2012, 87–89.

14. Amy Gross, "Your Brain on Happiness," *Newsweek*, January 16, 2012, 35.

15. Morten L. Kringelbach and Kent C. Berridge, "The Joyful Mind," *Scientific American*, August 2012, 45.

16. Lauren F. Friedman, "Eyes on the Prize," *Psychology Today*, January/February 2013, 9.

17. Friedman, "Eyes on the Prize."

18. Susan Graves, "Find Your Happiness," *Prevention*, January 2013, 104.

19. Jeffrey Kluger, Alex Aciman, and Katy Steinmetz, "The Happiness of Pursuit," *Time*, July 8, 2013, 24.

20. Statista.com; that number rose to 81 percent in 2017.

21. Kluger, Aciman, and Steinmetz, "The Happiness of Pursuit."

22. Kluger, Aciman, and Steinmetz, "The Happiness of Pursuit."

23. Andrea Sachs, "Come On, Get Happy," *Publishers Weekly*, October 20, 2014, 20.

24. Sachs, "Come On, Get Happy."

25. Alison Beard, "The Happiness Backlash," *Harvard Business Review*, July–August 2015, 130.

26. Beard, "The Happiness Backlash."

27. Beard, "The Happiness Backlash."

28. Mandy Oaklander, "Why Chasing Happiness Might Make You Miserable," *Time*, October 12, 2015, 28.

29. Jennifer Moss, "Happiness Isn't the Absence of Negative Feelings," *Harvard Business Review*, August 20, 2015, 1–5.

30. Moss, "Happiness Isn't the Absence of Negative Feelings."

31. Marie Bostwick, "Unfashionably Happy," *Publishers Weekly*, June 22, 2015, 144.

32. "Apps that Make You Happy," *Health*, May 2017, 10.

33. Clare McHugh, "Happy Begins Here," *Health*, March 2016, 6.

34. "Happy Money Launches Joy, the First Money App Powered by Psychology," *PR Newswire*, November 8, 2017.

35. Alyssa Kozak, "100 Days of Happiness Is a Social Media Craze," *University Wire*, February 14, 2017.

36. Laura Vanderkam, "A Generation for Likes," *Wall Street Journal*, February 14, 2017.

37. Tom Montgomery Fate, "The Ups and Downs of 'iGen'; Psychologist Ties Young People's Smartphone Use to Less Happiness," *The Baltimore Sun*, November 26, 2017, R2.

38. Camille Noe Pagan, "The (Real!) Secret to Happiness," *Health*, January/February 2016, 128.

39. Collin Binkley, "At Harvard's Newest Center, Researchers Look for Happiness," *St. Louis Post-Dispatch*, May 1, 2016, A5.

40. "Happiness Concentrator Selected as Gates Cambridge Scholar," *University Wire*, March 1, 2017.

41. David Shimer, "Easier Taught Than Done? Yale's Most Popular Class Tackles Happiness," *New York Times*, January 29, 2018, A19.

42. "56 Happy Billboards Put a Smile Across America for International Day of Happiness," *PR Newswire*, March 15, 2016.

43. "ProFlowers Celebrates International Day of Happiness by Gifting 10,000 Fresh Flowers to Unsuspecting Passers-By," *PR Newswire,* March 20, 2017.

44. "New Survey Finds Berries Are More Likely to Be Associated with Happiness Than Any Other Popular Fruit or Vegetable," *Business Wire*, August 31, 2016.

45. "Live Happy Magazine Features Jillian Michaels on Cover of January/February Issue," *PR Newswire*, January 5, 2016.

46. "Live Happy Invites All to Join the 'March to Happiness,'" *PR Newswire*, March 1, 2016.

47. "Creative Consultancy Lippincott Is Staging a Happiness Intervention at SXSW," *Business Wire*, March 7, 2016.

48. "Pennsylvania Tourism Office Unveils New Slogan and Logo Inviting Visitors to 'Pursue Your Happiness,'" *PR Newswire*, March 8, 2016.

49. "Forget Your Wedding Day or Even Having a Baby, Booking.com Research Reveals Travel Is the Secret to True Happiness," *PR Newswire*, November 29, 2016.

50. "StubHub Global Survey Finds Live Experiences Hold the Keys to Happiness," *Business Wire*, October 18, 2016.

51. "LG Launches 'Experience Happiness' Initiative," *PR Newswire*, November 29, 2017.

52. "Millennial Startup 'Naked Moment' Sells a Formula for Happiness," *PR Newswire*, June 9, 2017.

53. Alex Beam, "The Misery of Unrelenting Happiness," *Boston Globe*, February 22, 2016, A11.

54. Alan Ehrenhalt, "Should Governments Measure People's Happiness?" *TCA Regional News*, January 1, 2018.

55. Jenna Gallegos, "Buying Services Can Mean Buying Happiness. So Why Don't More People Do So?" *Washington Post*, July 25, 2017, A3.

56. Gene Epstein, "The Happiness Conundrum," *Barron's*, August 21, 2017, 20.

57. Husna Haq, "World Happiness Report: What Makes Some Countries Happier Than Others?" *The Christian Science Monitor*, March 16, 2016.

58. "The Smurfs on the Pursuit of Happiness," *Targeted News Service*, March 20, 2017.

59. Lucinda Shen, "Americans May Be Rich, But They're Not Happy," fortune.com, March 20, 2017.

60. Ryan Bort, "The Social Crisis Causing America's World Happiness Ranking to Plummet," newsweek.com, March 21, 2017.

61. "The Smurfs on the Pursuit of Happiness," *Targeted News Service*, March 20, 2017.

Epilogue

1. Anthony Seldon, *Beyond Happiness: The Trap of Happiness and How to Find Deeper Meaning and Joy* (London, UK: Yellow Kite, 2015); note that in his widely respected theory of emotions, Robert Plutchik states that humans have eight basic feelings: fear, anger, sadness, joy, disgust, surprise, trust, and anticipation. Plutchik makes no real distinction between joy and happiness, which is typical in the psychological fields of emotion and personality. See Robert Plutchik, "The Circumplex as a General Model of the Structure of Emotions and Personality," *American Psychological Association*, January 1, 1997, 17–45.

SELECTED
BIBLIOGRAPHY

Baker, Dan, and Cameron Stauth. *What Happy People Know: How the New Science of Happiness Can Change Your Life for the Better.* Emmaus, PA: Rodale, 2004.

Banks, Amy, and Leigh Ann Hirshman. *Four Ways to Click: Rewire Your Brain for Stronger, More Rewarding Relationships.* New York: TarcherPerigee, 2015.

Beck, Martha. *Finding Your Own North Star: Claiming the Life You Were Meant to Live.* New York: MJF Books, 2001.

Berg, Louis. *The Human Personality.* Upper Saddle River, NJ: Prentice Hall/Pearson Education, 1933.

Bok, Derek. *The Politics of Happiness: What Government Can Learn from the New Research on Well-Being.* Princeton, NJ: Princeton University Press, 2010.

Bok, Sissela. *Exploring Happiness: From Aristotle to Brain Science.* New Haven, CT: Yale University Press, 2010.

Brande, Dorothea. *Wake Up and Live!* Chicago: Justin Brande & Gilbert J. Collins, 1936.

Cadman, S. Parkes. *Adventure for Happiness.* New York: The Macmillan Company, 1935.

Callwood, June. *Love, Hate, Fear, Anger and the Other Lively Emotions.* New York: Doubleday, 1964.

Carter, Christine. *The Sweet Spot: How to Find Your Groove at Home and Work.* New York: Ballantine Books, 2015.

Csikszentmihalyi, Mihaly. *Flow: The Psychology of Optimal Experience.* New York: Harper & Row, 1990.

————. *Finding Flow*. New York: Basic Books, 1997.

Davies, William. *The Happiness Industry: How the Government and Big Business Sold Us Well-Being*. New York: Verso Books, 2015.

Dearden, Harold. *Understanding Ourselves: The Fine Art of Happiness*. New York: Boni & Liveright, 1926.

de Botton, Alain. *Status Anxiety*. New York: Pantheon, 2004.

de Man, Henri. *Joy in Work*. London: Allen & Unwin, 1929.

Diener, Ed, and Robert Biswas-Diener, *Happiness: Unlocking the Mysteries of Psychological Wealth*. Hoboken, NJ: Wiley-Blackwell, 2008.

Dunn, Elizabeth, and Michael Norton. *Happy Money: The New Science of Smarter Spending*. New York: Simon & Schuster, 2013.

Dworkin, Ronald W. *Artificial Happiness: The Dark Side of the New Happy Class*. New York: Carroll & Graf, 2006.

Dyer, Wayne. *Your Erroneous Zones*. New York: Funk & Wagnalls, 1976.

Ehrenreich, Barbara. *Bright-Sided: How Relentless Promotion of Positive Thinking Has Undermined America*. New York: Metropolitan Books/Henry Holt & Company, 2009.

Ferrero, Gina Lombroso. *The Soul of Woman*. New York: E. P. Dutton, 1923.

Foster, Rick, and Greg Hicks. *How We Choose to Be Happy: The 9 Choices of Extremely Happy People—Their Secrets, Their Stories*. New York: Putnam Adult, 1999.

Freedman, Jonathan. *Happy People*. New York: Harcourt Brace Jovanovich, 1978.

Freitas, Donna. *The Happiness Effect: How Social Media Is Driving a Generation to Appear Perfect at Any Cost*. New York: Oxford University Press, 2017.

Fromm, Erich. *Man for Himself: An Inquiry into the Psychology of Ethics*. New York: Rinehart and Company, 1947.

————. *The Sane Society*. New York: Rinehart and Company, 1955.

Gaylin, Willard. *Feelings: Our Vital Signs*. New York: Harper and Row, 1979.

Gilbert, Daniel. *Stumbling on Happiness*. New York: Alfred A. Knopf, 2006.

Gilkey, James Gordan. *Here Is Help for You*. New York: Macmillan, 1951.

Goodspeed, Edgar J. *Buying Happiness*. Chicago: University of Chicago Press, 1933.

Gorman, William, and Mortimer Adler. *The American Testament*. Chicago: William Benton, Encyclopedia Britannica, 1976.

Graham, Billy. *The Secret of Happiness*. New York: Doubleday, 1955.

Graham, Carol. *Happiness around the World: The Paradox of Happy Peasants and Miserable Millionaires*. New York: Oxford University Press, 2010.

Greenbie, Marjorie Barstow. *In Quest of Contentment*. New York: Whittlesey House, 1936.

Gruenberg, Sidonie M., and Hilda Sidney Grech. *The Many Lives of Modern Woman: A Guide to Happiness in Her Complex Role*. New York: Doubleday, 1952.

Gumpert, Martin. *You Are Younger Than You Think*. New York: Duell, Sloan and Pearce, 1944.

Hazleton, Lesley. *The Right to Feel Bad: Coming to Terms with Normal Depression*. Garden City, NY: Doubleday, 1984.

Heisz, Deborah. *Live Happy: Ten Practices for Choosing Joy*. New York: HarperElixir, 2016.

His Holiness the Dalai Lama and Howard C. Cutler. *The Art of Happiness: A Handbook for Living*. New York: Riverhead Books, 1998.

Hotep, I. M. *Love and Happiness*. New York: Alfred A. Knopf, 1938.

Jones, Howard Mumford. *The Pursuit of Happiness*. Cambridge, MA: Harvard University Press, 1953.

Kahneman, Daniel, Ed Diener, and Norbert Schwarz. *Well-Being: The Foundations of Hedonistic Psychology of Hedonistic Psychology*. New York: Russell Sage Foundation, 1999.

Kashdan, Todd, and Robert Biswas-Diener. *The Upside of Your Dark Side: Why Being Your Whole Self—Not Just Your "Good" Self—Drives Success and Fulfillment*. New York: Hudson Street Press, 2014.

Kasser, Tim. *The High Price of Materialism*. Cambridge, MA: The MIT Press, 2002.

Kiley, John Kantwell. *Self-Rescue*. New York: McGraw-Hill, 1977.

Kingwell, Mark. *Better Living: In Pursuit of Happiness from Plato to Prozac*. Toronto: Penguin Canada, 1998.

Klein, Stefan. *The Science of Happiness: How Our Brains Make Us Happy—and What We Can Do to Get Happier*. Cambridge, MA: Da Capo Press, 2006.

Kushner, Harold. *When All You've Ever Wanted Isn't Enough: The Search for a Life That Matters*. New York: Summit Books, 1986.

Lapham, Roger F. *It's in Your Power*. New York: Duell, Sloan and Pearce, 1947.

Layard, Richard. *Happiness: Lessons from a New Science*. New York: Penguin, 2005.

Leland, John. *Happiness Is a Choice You Make: Lessons from a Year Among the Oldest Old*. New York: Sarah Crichton Books, 2018.

Lelord, François. *Hector and the Search for Happiness*. New York: Penguin, 2010.

MacIver, R. M. *The Pursuit of Happiness: A Philosophy for Modern Living*. New York: Simon & Schuster, 1955.

McGonigal, Kelly. *The Upside of Stress: Why Stress Is Good for You, and How to Get Good at It*. New York: Penguin, 2015.

McMahon, Darrin M. *Happiness: A History*. New York: Atlantic Monthly Press, 2005.

Murray, Charles. *In Pursuit of Happiness and Good Government*. New York: Simon & Schuster, 1988.

Newman, Mildred, and Bernard Berkowitz. *How to Be Your Own Best Friend*. New York: Random House, 1971.

Oettingen, Gabriele. *Rethinking Positive Thinking: Inside the New Science of Motivation*. New York: Penguin Random House, 2014.

Packard, Vance. *The Status Seekers*. New York: David McKay, 1959.

Pasricha, Neil. *The Happiness Equation: Want Nothing + Do Anything = Have Everything*. New York: G. P. Putnam's Sons, 2016.

Peale, Norman Vincent. *The Power of Positive Thinking*. New York: Prentice-Hall, 1952.

Peale, Norman Vincent, and Smiley Blanton. *The Art of Real Happiness*. New York: Prentice-Hall, 1950.

Pitkin, Walter A. *The Psychology of Happiness*. New York: Simon & Schuster, 1929.

Pittman, Walter. *Life Begins at 40*. New York: McGraw-Hill Company, 1932.

Potter, Charles Francis. *Technique of Happiness*. New York: Macaulay, 1935.

Powell, John. *Happiness Is an Inside Job*. Allen, TX: Thomas More Association, 1989.

Powys, John Cowper. *The Art of Happiness*. New York: Simon & Schuster, 1935.

Reiss, Steven. *Who Am I? The 16 Basic Desires That Motivate Our Happiness and Define Our Personalities*. New York: Tarcher/Putnam, 2000.

Ricard, Matthieu. *Happiness: A Guide to Developing Life's Most Important Skill*. New York: Little, Brown, 2006.

Robson, William A. *The Relation of Wealth to Welfare*. New York: Macmillan Company, 1925.

Rodale, Ardath H., *Climbing Toward the Light: A Journey of Growth, Understanding, and Love*. Emmaus, PA: Good Spirit Press, 1989.

Roueche, Berton. *The Delectable Mountains*. Boston: Little, Brown, 1959.

Rubin, Gretchen. *The Happiness Project: Or, Why I Spent a Year Trying to Sing in the Morning, Clean My Closets, Fight Right, Read Aristotle, and Generally Have More Fun*. New York: Harper, 2009.

Russell, Bertrand. *The Conquest of Happiness*. New York: Liveright, 1930.

Samuel, Lawrence R. *Supernatural America: A Cultural History*. Santa Barbara, CA: Praeger, 2011.

——. *The American Dream: A Cultural History*. Syracuse, NY: Syracuse University Press, 2012.

——. *The American Middle Class: A Cultural History*. New York: Routledge, 2013.

——. *Shrink: A Cultural History of Psychoanalysis in America*. Lincoln: University of Nebraska Press, 2013.

——. *The American Way of Life: A Cultural History*. Madison, NJ: Fairleigh Dickinson University Press, 2017.

Schiddel, Edmund. *The Devil in Bucks County*. New York: Simon & Schuster, 1959.

Seldon, Anthony. *Beyond Happiness: The Trap of Happiness and How to Find Deeper Meaning and Joy*. London, UK: Yellow Kite, 2015.

Seligman, Martin. *Learned Optimism*. New York: Alfred A. Knopf, 1991.

——. *Authentic Happiness: Using the New Positive Psychology to Realize Your Potential for Lasting Fulfillment*. New York: Free Press, 2002.

Shaw, Charles Gray. *The Road to Happiness*. New York: Hillman-Curl, 1937.

Sheen, Fulton J. *Way to Happiness: A Guide to Peace, Hope and Contentment.* Garden City, NY: Garden City Books, 1954.

Sokoloff, Boris. *The Achievement of Happiness.* New York: Simon & Schuster, 1935.

Stearns, Peter N. *Satisfaction Not Guaranteed: Dilemmas of Progress in Modern Society.* New York: NYU Press, 2012.

Strack, Fritz, Michael Argyle, and Norbert Schwarz, eds., *Subjective Well-Being: An Interdisciplinary Perspective.* Oxford, UK: Pergamon Press, 1991.

Tiger, Lionel. *Optimism: The Biology of Hope.* New York: Simon & Schuster, 1979.

Twenge, Jean M. *iGen: Why Today's Super-Connected Kids Are Growing Up Less Rebellious, More Tolerant, Less Happy—and Completely Unprepared for Adulthood—and What That Means for the Rest of Us.* New York: Atria Books, 2017.

van Praag, Bernard, and Ada Ferrer-i-Carbonell. *Happiness Quantified: A Satisfaction Calculus Approach.* New York: Oxford University Press, 2004.

Wachtel, Paul L. *The Poverty of Affluence: A Psychological Portrait of the American Way of Life.* New York: Free Press, 1983.

Wakefield, Jerome, and Allan Horwitz. *The Loss of Sadness: How Psychiatry Transformed Normal Sorrow Into Depressive Disorder.* New York: Oxford University Press, 2006.

White, Nicholas P. *A Brief History of Happiness.* Hoboken, NJ: Wiley-Blackwell, 2006.

Wholey, Dennis. *Are You Happy? Some Answers to the Most Important Question in Your Life.* New York: Houghton Mifflin Harcourt, 1986.

Wiley, Bell. *So You're Going to Get Married.* Philadelphia: J. B. Lippincott & Company, 1938.

Wills, Garry. *Inventing America: Jefferson's Declaration of Independence.* New York: Doubleday, 1978.

Wilson, Eric. *Against Happiness: In Praise of Melancholy.* New York: Farrar, Strauss and Giroux, 2008.

Wilson, Sloan. *The Man in the Gray Flannel Suit.* New York: Simon & Schuster, 1955.

Winkler, Alan M. *Home Front U.S.A.: America during World War II.* Wheeling, IL: Harlan Davidson, 2012.

Yutang, Lin. *On the Wisdom of America.* New York: J. Day, 1950.

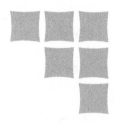

INDEX

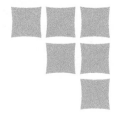

ABOUT THE AUTHOR

Lawrence R. Samuel is the founder of AmeriCulture, a Miami- and New York–based consultancy dedicated to translating the emerging cultural landscape into business opportunities. Larry has been a leading culture consultant to Fortune 500 companies and blue-chip advertising agencies since 1990 and, as one of the top trend consultants in the country, he advised a Who's Who of companies and agencies across a wide variety of industries and categories. Larry's breakthrough research study on American wealth culture for J. P. Morgan, which identified five types of American millionaires based on his unique methodology rooted in cultural anthropology, was widely reported in the media. Larry is a blogger for *Psychology Today*, where he has received hundreds of thousands of hits. He holds a PhD in American studies from the University of Minnesota and is the author of many books, including *Freud on Madison Avenue: Motivation Research and Subliminal Advertising in America* (Univeristy of Pennsylvania, 2010); *Sexidemic: A Cultural History of Sex in America* (Rowman & Littlefield, 2013); *Shrink: A Cultural History of Psychoanalysis in America* (University of Nebraska, 2013); *Death, American Style: A Cultural History of Dying in America* (Rowman & Littlefield, 2013); *American Fatherhood: A Cultural History* (Rowman & Littlefield, 2016); and *Aging in America: A Cultural History* (University of Pennsylvania, 2017).